How to Become a Great Software Developer and Produce High Quality Code: Roadmap

Noura Bensaber

Dedication

To my family, to the spirit of my dear father and to my beloved husband Kamel.

Table of Contents

General Introduction

Developing high-quality software is a challenge. The software systems and their code base should evolve for increasingly demanding customers that do not stop asking for more and more functionalities. Work environments (programming languages, testing tools, deployment tools, etc.) are steadily becoming more complex. Moreover, IT concepts are complicated and require resilience, patience, discipline, and hard work to be understood. As a software developer, you should be cross-functional to be ready to work independently and in a team. You should be proactive and highly motivated. You must have abstract and analytical thinking and master the required concepts.

Don't give up so easily. It sounds like mission impossible, but it's not. You just need to have the plan to get the tools to start and follow your journey as a developer with confidence and peace of mind. But, you can spend years completing some tasks, unaware there are ways to help you accomplish them better and in less time. When programming, you may have many doubts and ask yourself many questions. How can I better break down my program into modules and classes? What is missing in my code to be secure?

That's why I decided to write this book to answer these kinds of questions and to save you from wasting time identifying tools or techniques that help you to be a great developer. I have collected for you in this book as many techniques as possible to help you quickly improve your learning and development processes. For example, I will describe guidelines like architectural rules and recommendations to orient you on how you split your code into parts like modules and classes. I'll talk about techniques to follow and tools to use to keep your code secure. Instead of spending perhaps years to be able to access such information, read this book.

This book is a kind of toolbox describing several theoretical concepts as well as many techniques to serve as a guide to unleash the productivity of software developers and improve the quality of their code. This book aims to draw attention to many little and big things you might overlook, but they are often the key to developing a product of top quality.

This book is implicitly divided into two parts. The first aims to remind you of the most crucial ideas to improve certain aspects of your personality, such as focus, memory, communication skills, or your learning process. As you are ready and willing

1

to develop software, we continue, in the second part, the journey by preparing you with multiple ideas, techniques, and even tips. All this will help you learn how to produce high-level programming code while optimizing cost and development time.

Why is code quality so important? Quality is the concluding criterion of a product for its shipment and deployment. In my opinion, high-quality code, from good architecture to correct statements, is a solid platform for the success of any IT business. If the product code is readable, extensible, and with weak coupling between its different components, then changes, corrections of issues, extensions, or adding new features are straightforward. Moreover, you spare a lot of time, and the clients are satisfied! They get what they want by the deadline.

We briefly resume some of what we present in this book as material to help you take steps forward in writing better code.

We will define the main code quality aspects like readability and extensibility and what techniques and concepts you should learn to improve them.

We will talk about concepts like software architecture, design patterns, and SOLID principles to boost your object-oriented thinking and modeling. We will show through examples, how these concepts ameliorate code aspects like maintainability, flexibility, reusability, etc. We will share some best practices with you to improve processes like continuous integration/continuous delivery etc.

Code problems, especially security issues, lead to high costs if you do not eliminate them. We will illustrate it with examples. We will present the standard rules and recommendations you should follow and the tools you should use to address these risks.

The IDE (Integrated Development Editor) you use to develop your application has a tremendous impact on the quality of your code thanks to the options it offers, such as the possibility of analyzing your code or shortcuts to speed up your coding. That's why we devote a chapter to explaining what the most popular IDEs offer you as possibilities to improve the quality of your code. We also clarify how you can exploit all these options to save a lot of time while coding.

Processes such as unit testing and debugging are necessary to improve the quality of your code. They help identify what went wrong and whether your code meets its requirements. To show you the effect of these tools on the quality of your code, we'll explain unit testing using JUnit as a sample and an example of a Java program. We will show you how to debug your code using Intellij Idea and a Java program as an example of back-end debugging. We'll also show you how to perform front-end debugging using Chrome DevTools. We'll also give you some best practices you can follow to improve your logging, etc.

Finally, we will afford some best practices for Java and JQuery. We restrict ourselves to only these languages for simplicity reasons.

By the end of reading this book, you will have a series of techniques to follow that will help you organize yourself to learn well and increase your coding productivity level. On the other hand, it depends on the area in which you want to specialize. You have to dive deep into learning in this area. This book is a general roadmap to open your eyes to consider and apply all known factors to produce a code of high quality.

This book is structured into seven chapters, the content of each of which will be described individually:

Chapter 1: Better Learning Process.

Chapter 2: How to Become a Better Developer.

Chapter 3: Software Development and Code Quality.

Chapter 4: Code Issues and how to Fix Them.

Chapter 5: IDEs and Code Quality.

Chapter 6: Processes and Techniques for Better Code Quality.

Chapter 7: Programming Tips for Better Code Quality.

Chapter 1: Better Learning Process

1. Introduction

As the private life you lead has a tremendous impact on the quality of your learning, we allowed ourselves to advise you to make changes in your daily life. These changes help you improve aspects, like increasing your mental capabilities, focus, or physical vitality. This process is necessary for better comprehension and memorization of what you learn. Further training should be a regular ritual for a junior or senior developer. To be a productive developer, you must identify your strengths and weaknesses and focus mainly on the latter to reduce or eliminate them.

So, we want to present, in this chapter, some ideas that could help you improve your learning process. But before that, we'll introduce some techniques that have proven their effectiveness in significantly improving how to learn quickly and efficiently.

2. How to Learn more Effectively

To stay competitive, you should always learn new things. The first meta-skill to learn is how to learn quickly and efficiently. It has been proven that there are ways to learn quickly and to memorize what we learn effectively. Here we introduce the various well-known methods that help significantly to improve your learning process.

2.1. Teach (or Pretend) Someone Else

You can speed up your learning and remember more if you teach someone else or pretend. Expectation changes the mindset so that you have more effective approaches to learning than those who do it passively.

One way to implement this idea is to give your teammates a one-hour presentation (or example. weekly or monthly) on the topic you are learning. In this case, you will receive feedback and questions from them. That will make your brain better grasp information.

2.2. Learning in Short Times and Taking Breaks

A better learning process consists of learning in sessions with short breaks. According to studies, it is recommended to learn in a 50-minute session and then take a break of 5-10 minutes. Learning for more than 50 minutes without stopping becomes a burden on the brain. You don't have to keep track of time to the minute, but do what suits you better. So, you can study for each session, in time intervals of 50 minutes to 1 hour, a little bit shorter than 50 minutes, or longer if you're still in your flow state.

But do not keep learning for hours. You should stop and take a short break (5 to 10 minutes). During this break, you can, for example, have a coffee, read your email, or go to the toilet. That often helps to cope with stress. Keep in mind that the basic idea is to break up your learning sessions with well-timed short breaks to refresh your mind and manage your stress before continuing.

2.3. Writing Notes

It is known that handwriting notes help us listen more actively and identify important concepts. But whatever the means, taking notes is usually good anyway. Technological progress allows us to have other tools for taking notes. We sum up some points that you can follow to take notes as follows:

- Write with pen and paper or other devices you use like mobile or laptop. You can use whatever method or technology you feel comfortable with.

- Take screenshots by using available tools like Snipping Tool, LightShot, etc.

- If possible, take photos and videos with a smartphone.

- Study actively by summarizing what you learn in your own words. That gives you a better chance of not forgetting what you have learned.

- Process information immediately or a little bit later.

- Don't hesitate to ask questions if you are in a situation where the teacher is present live or online.

2.4. Learning in a Variety of Ways

To learn a skill, you need to use different methods. Sometimes, watching a video helps you learn faster than reading a tutorial. But it is good to mix different ways to learn the same topic.

2.5. Space Effect

Memory is necessary for learning, but unfortunately, we often forget rapidly! To not quickly forget what you have learned, you can use powerful learning techniques to counteract the natural rate of forgetting. It's about getting the concepts right. Then, use memorization and spaced repetition techniques to retain the information.

2.5.1. Understanding the Concepts Well

To memorize a particular topic better, you need to understand the concepts of that topic very well. That leads to strong primary memory.

2.5.2. Memorization Techniques

We do not know if you will need all these techniques or a few of them to be a developer. But we want to describe them to inform you that they exist and they help retain information.

2.5.2.1. Mind Maps

Mind mapping is a visual way to organize your ideas (tasks, concepts, etc.) for better understanding and recall. When you create a mind map, you start from a central idea and extend it with related topics to draw a tree structure. Using different colors, shapes, and images will generate a highly structured, intuitive, and easy-to-remember diagram. There are many platforms today (free or not) that you can use to create mind maps. The Miro board tool is one of them.

2.5.2.2. Mnemonics Devices

Mnemonic devices are memory techniques that help increase your ability to retain and retrieve information. They allow converting information from short-term memory to long-term memory. Mnemonic devices are classified into different types that we want to share with you:

Acronyms and acrostics: an acronym is a word made up of the first letter of each word in a set of words you want to remember. The word ROYGBIV is a well-known acronym for the colors of the rainbow: **r**ed, **o**range, **y**ellow, **g**reen, **b**lue, **i**ndigo, and **v**iolet.

On the other hand, an acrostic is a phrase made up of the first letter of each word in a group of words you want to memorize. A known example of acrostics is the sentence: '**M**y **V**ery **E**ducated **M**other **J**ust **S**ent **U**s **N**ine **P**izzas' which helps you remember the nine planets as they are ordered in the solar system: **M**ercury, **V**enus, **E**arth, **M**ars, **J**upiter, **S**aturn, **U**ranus, **N**eptune, and **P**luto.

Association: you can store information for easier retrieval if you link it to something you already know well. It could be a phrase or an image.

Chunking: this technique suggests storing information by breaking it down into small pieces called 'chunks'. The chunks are easy to retain and recall because they are tiny. You can use this technique to remember information like phone numbers. Instead of memorizing the whole number, you can break it into pieces. Each piece is composed of 3 digits.

Songs and rhymes: using music is an effective way to retain information in long-term memory. When you convert data into a song or a poem, you will have great power to memorize it. The song "A-B-C" is a well-known example of using music to retain information.

Method of loci: the method of loci, also called the 'memory palace technique', uses locations to memorize items or ideas. The word loci is Latin, and it is the plural of the word locus, which means 'location'. You can take the following steps to use this technique:

- Close your eyes and imagine a space that you are very familiar with, like your house or office.

- Define a route and walk through the different locations on this path in your imagination. For example, if your path is home, your location could be a doorway, hallway, living room, etc.

- Link each item (from the group of items you want to remember) to each location. It will be better if you create a silly or exaggerated mental image for the item.

- When you walk through the locations in the sequence and the same order, you will retrieve your items from your memory.

2.5.3. Spaced Repetition

This technique promotes the idea that repetitions are essential for learning and retaining information in long-term memory. It introduces time intervals (like one day, three days, etc.) between learning units. For example, you learn a new subject on the first day, and after the end of the first time interval (one day), you review this theme. You wait three days (the second time slot) to do your second repetition to learn the subject, and so on. That way, you'll understand and retain the topic well, even if you spend fewer hours learning it.

2.6. Be Focused and Aware

Use the period in which you have your best concentration. You can also train yourself to be in the flow state because when you get it, you will lose track of time and feel focused, happy, innovative, and productive. But when you lose focus because something is bothering you and stressing you out, or your brain starts to wander, there are some tips to follow to overcome these situations.

For things that stress you out (like problems to solve), schedule them later such saying, I'll take care of this problem the next day. You will find some peace and forget about those worries, at least temporarily, to focus on your learning process.

For the things that make you dream, what can help is reminding yourself how important what you learn is for you and how your career will be stagnated if you do not improve yourself. How much time did you waste, and how much time will you waste? Then, convince yourself how this will make you progress in your work or life. Gain motivation and bring back your ability and strength to focus and push forward to master what you are doing.

2.7. Eliminate Distractions

Reacting to every notification from your mobile will distract you from focusing on your learning process. Get rid of these distractions by switching off your smartphone if necessary, show yourself busy in Skype and MS Teams if you use these tools, and so on.

2.8. Learning Environment

Prepare and maintain your learning environment to be ergonomic, well-lighted, and   calm.

2.9. Setting Goals

Set a goal (topic to master) and schedule learning it. You have to know the prerequisites of the subject you need to master. If you do not meet a precondition, you must first acquire knowledge on this subtopic.

2.10. Learning Techniques

Choose and diversify your learning techniques like videos, tutorials, or online courses.

2.11. Interleaving

Studies have shown that people can learn and remember new concepts better when they switch between a few different topics or practices instead of learning only one theme.

2.12. Avoid Learning in Random Way

Learning randomly, in many cases, leads you to miss essential parts and creates knowledge gaps. So, you cannot take advantage of what you learned correctly. You will always struggle when you use it. Hence, structure your learning methodologically by following the coming schema:

- Define the topic you want to learn.

- Get the necessary material to learn the topic, like videos, tutorials, subscriptions to a course, etc.

- Start by getting an overview of it, like looking for the main definitions (what is about it?), the advantages, the disadvantages, and a comparison with other similar topics.

- Now dive into the details and start at the beginner level. Use spacing and repetition techniques until you master the main concepts. Then upgrade to the intermediate level, and when you master it, go to the expert level.

2.13. Use Pomodoro Technique

This technique is so popular and known as a time management method. It encourages you to alternate between focused work sessions and short breaks to reduce the mental load for further sustained concentration. To practice this technique, follow the coming steps:

- Choose a task.
- Set a timer for 25 minutes.
- Take a 5 minutes break.
- Take a prolonged break after four sessions.

You can use this technique if it suits you better. You can also alternate learning sessions (for example, 50-minute sessions) and breaks as described above.

3. Habits and Work-Life Balance

A work-life balance such as good sleep, a healthy diet, adequate fluid intake (drinking enough water), and enjoying your hobbies during your leisure time relax you, reduce your stress, and help you learn effectively. Taking rest helps clear your head for efficient learning and information memorizing.

3.1. Healthy Eating Plan and Exercise

To set a healthy eating plan, consult here [16] and [17] on the list of healthy foods. But we want to advise you to check regularly that your body has enough vitamins like magnesium, zinc, iron, and vitamin E. The first two vitamins are good for mood. Magnesium and iron give you energy and vitality, and vitamin E reduces the effect of brain aging. Moreover, we want to advise you to reduce your sugar intake. Taking a quantity of sugar more than what is allowed will make your brain foggy and less concentrated.

Physical activities have many benefits, including improving thinking and learning skills. If you are already athletic and go to gyms, this is great for you. Otherwise, you will find here [18] the recommended physical activities in your case. In the worst case, keep walking for at least ten minutes a day and several times a week.

Overwork can be dangerous. It can cause burnout and kill your ambition and will to pursue your goals. Extra fatigue increases the incident rate.

3.2. Improving Quality Sleep

Studies show that regular and good-quality sleep enhances brain performance, mood, productivity, and overall health. For most adults, at least seven or more hours of sleep each night are recommended. If you're having trouble getting a good night's sleep, there are some very efficient rules to follow to help you sleep better:

- Your bedroom should be dedicated solely to sleep. No electronic devices like computers, cell phones, or television should be in your bedroom.

- Your bedroom should be dark enough, noiseless, and at a comfortable temperature.

- Your bed should be comfortable and make you feel good.

- Your sleep should be regular. Go to bed at the same time every night (ideally 10 pm as studies suggest) and get up at the same time every morning, also on weekends. It will regulate your biological clock.

- Stop at 4 pm consuming stimulants like caffeine and sugar.

- When you go to bed, close your eyes, try to sleep, and do nothing else. You train your brain to shut down every time you go to bed. If you can't sleep for 20 minutes, go to another room and do soothing things like reading or listening to soft music.

3.3. Automaticity

If you feel overwhelmed, don't have enough time to learn, and that other tasks are taking up too much of your time and effort, it's time to clean up and organize your life. Several studies have attested that up to 50% of what we do is a habit. In other words, we do it automatically. Sleeping, eating, taking showers, or brushing our teeth are examples of routines that we perform daily. More automaticity in your life will help you achieve what you have planned for a day or a week to avoid too much tiredness and even burnout. Indeed, we make automatic actions with barely thinking or having conflicts to make decisions, which reduces mental load and decision fatigue.

But, such actions should be good habits and not bad ones. For more details about this topic, you can read the best sellers' books in this domain like [1], [2], and [3] to get help to replace bad habits (if you have some) with good ones. But, we still present on the fly some ideas to follow to lower your mental load.

3.3.1. Delegate Decisions

It is impossible to do everything by yourself. To reduce your mental and physical loads, you have to delegate some of your tasks to others. These others could be family members or a service that you pay for. Examples of services you pay for are cleaning up or online shopping with home delivery.

3.3.2. Daily Routines for Simple Tasks

Avoid confusion about known tasks and have an accurate daily and weekly plan. Having a plan will create some automaticity to put certain decisions on autopilot. It reduces decision fatigue, simplifies your options, saves time, and simplifies your daily life. Some examples of these routines that you can fix their time are:

- When you exercise.

- When you do your shopping.

- When you cook at home and which meal on which day.

- When you eat in a restaurant, when you order.

- Organize your closet so that you can easily pick up your items to wear and prepare tomorrow's outfit the day before.

3.3.3. Take Fewer Decisions

To make fewer decisions, you can follow some tips:

- Write the list of what you need to buy and schedule your next shopping in a rotating way.

- Make a to-do list of what you want to do in the next few days or on weekends, and set a time for that.

- Prioritize daily choices. If your list is too long, achieve at least the most important ones.

- Create automaticity for trivial tasks like exercise, time with family, or reading a book.

- Do affirmations like saying, I will finish this task and take care of that one. Affirmations help you boost your self-confidence and determination to take action. It helps overcome your negative self-talk.

3.4. Do Meditation

Many think that meditation is a complex practice. But this is not true. Some forms of meditation are simple. Many of us can exercise them to reap many benefits, including overcoming the problem of losing focus when the mind starts to wander. Other benefits of meditation are increasing concentration, reducing stress and anxiety, and enhancing moods and quality of sleep. That's why we decided to add a brief description of one of the simplest forms of meditation:

Take a seat: find a place calm and quiet for you. Take a seat that you feel stable and can comfortably stay in that position for some time. Choose the most convenient position for you. You can sit in a chair or couch with your feet on the floor or on a yoga mat cross-legged.

Set a time: set a short time, like 5 or 10 minutes, if this is new for you.

Get started: relax and close your eyes.

Follow your breath: start breathing in and breathing out. The main point is to focus on your breath as it goes in and out and avoid thinking about anything. But, if your mind starts to wander somewhere, bring it back and focus again on your breath.

3.5. Avoid Multitasking

Working on multiple tasks at the same time seems to be attractive at first glance, to get as much done as possible. But in fact, multitasking is mostly a productivity killer. Researches show that multitasking decreases concentration, understanding, and performance. As you perform many tasks simultaneously, your attention jumps from activity to activity, which forces you to stop thinking about one activity and refocus on another repeatedly. Moreover, switching actions between tasks demands extra time and effort from you. This process will distract and exhaust you. In the end, you won't complete any task satisfactorily because you missed concentration on any of those tasks. One more thing, multitasking does not allow you to reach your flow state, which is the best time to do a job perfectly.

3.6. Overcome Procrastination

Procrastination is the tendency to put off what you could do now, like waiting until tomorrow for what you could do today. The known causes of procrastination could be low self-esteem, lack of confidence, concentration problems, fear of failure, or the pursuit of perfectionism. A procrastinator thinks that it is too painful to perform such an action.

The consequences of procrastination are pervasive because you have always unfinished tasks waiting to be completed. It will be for your a source of stress, anxiety, guilt, and daily penalizing emotions. It will also distract you to do other tasks and even lead to bad sleep. To get rid of procrastination, you can follow the Zeigarnik Effect method that we sum up in a few steps as follows:

Make a to-do list: write down everything you need to do and schedule when and how to do it. Having a list with some details (time and way) helps you feel that things are easier to achieve because you have a roadmap of clear and direct actions to execute.

Start with a small step: make the first move and complete a small piece of your task. As mentioned earlier, your brain will remind you that your task is not finished. So, you know that you should perform another part of it until you complete it.

Split the overall task into small ones: breaking the task into small parts will encourage you to act because each piece will not take too much endeavor and time from you. So, you will hurry up to complete it and maybe stimulate your appetite to do the next one.

Never forget that procrastination is no more than a choice. It is up to you to make decisions.

4. Self-Learning Recommendations Resume

Several tools are available nowadays to help you learn alone or by taking lessons. Here are some tips to follow when self-learning:

- Read the documentation available at the level of the company (Wiki like Confluence) where you work, for example.

- Watch videos (open/paid) (e.g, Youtube, online learning and teaching platforms).

- Read tutorials and books.

- Blogs (e.g, Stackoverflow, Github, etc.):

    o Passive: taking advantage of answers that already exist.

    o Active: post questions and wait for answers or answer other people's questions.

- Participate in programming competitions.

- Discuss topics you learn with teammates.

- Do a lot of practice (programming and writing unit tests).

- Create side projects and push them to programming platforms like GitHub,   etc.

Chapter 2: How to Become a Better Developer

1. Introduction

Many powerful techniques are available to improve your cognitive and problem-solving skills. In this chapter, we introduce some key points that can help you to unlock your potential, improve your skills, and make you a better software developer. These points involve the engineering mindset, including improving your communication skills to collaborate well with your teammates, learning from your mistakes, and how to be more innovative. We'll also suggest other ideas, like how to solidify your knowledge and why it's better to develop your code on your own instead of overdoing it by copying other people's code. We'll detail these and other guidelines in the coming sections.

2. Engineering Mindset (The Way Engineers think)

To be a good software developer, you must have dedication and passion. You should be ready to pay the price by investing time and energy to become masterful. It takes concentrated effort to have a clear vision of what you want to achieve and a plan for it.

In addition to dedication and passion, there are eight main characteristics that people who are successful at solving problems of all kinds should have. These main qualities are part of the engineering mindset. We'll describe them in the coming section.

2.1. Curiosity

You must be thirsty to acquire new knowledge and skills, as software development tools are changing rapidly. We can recommend a way to keep you up to date so you don't miss learning what you need. While chatting with your teammates, watching a video, or even an advertisement, you hear about a concept you don't know. Then immediately go and look for its definition. If you find this concept interesting for your work, start planning to learn it.

2.2. Collaboration

By definition, collaboration is teamwork based on the individual work of each team member for a common goal to achieve commercial benefit.

You have to put in mind that software development is essentially a team effort and not an alone walk-through. Don't think you can do it all on your own. You have to work and share tasks with others.

2.3. Communication

As mentioned above, you have no choice but to collaborate with colleagues (developer, product owner, stakeholder, etc.) to achieve the overall goal of developing software. It is paramount that you prepare yourself with communication skills. But what are communication skills, and how can you improve them? Before that, let's remember that there are four main types of communication, that we use daily. We present in the following section a brief definition of each of them.

2.3.1. Types of Communication

The four known types of communication are:

Verbal: Communication is based on spoken language, like direct talking or phone calls.

Nonverbal: communication is based on body language.

Written: communication is based on written language.

Visual: communication is based on drawings.

2.3.2. Communication Skills

Here are some points that allow you to communicate well with your interlocutors. It helps you quickly and accurately understand the information exchanged and avoid frustrations and misunderstandings.

2.3.2.1. Active Listening

Listen carefully to your interlocutor, do not forget to ask questions, and even rephrase if necessary. It helps build trust and comprehension inside the team.

2.3.2.2. Communication Method

Choose the best communication method according to the circumstances and your interlocutor. Inside your developing team, foster the use of verbal communication. However, the explosion of the home office and the use of the video-conferences can lead to a combination of multiple methods (for example, verbal and written). On another side, if you are looking for a job, it is generally not appropriate to go looking for the boss of a company to apply for a job offer but to send a formal e-mail.

2.3.2.3. Confidence

It is one of the strongest skills you should have. You have to be very confident and sure of yourself when you speak. People have a tendency to respond much more to a person with high self-confidence.

2.3.2.4. Clarity and Simplicity

It's not about showing others how good you are at your spoken language. Try always to speak a language understandable by others so that you successfully get the message across.

2.3.2.5. Behavior: Kindness, Respect and Empathy

It's always good to be friendly when communicating with others. You can reinforce that kindness by asking interlocutors questions like: how are you? Or, how was your party yesterday? Or, your vacation?

Be respectful, and don't speak too loudly or too quietly. Be punctual to meetings, don't talk to others during someone's speech, and don't make fun of other people's ideas. Stay objective and listen to others and discuss their ideas the same way you want them to listen to you and discuss yours.

Understand and take into account the emotions of others and get ready to answer them with a suitable response. For example, if someone is frustrated, try to calm them down by giving them advice. If someone has new ideas and is excited to turn them over, try to encourage them or discuss objectively with them if something is impossible to perform.

Above all, you must avoid being seen as someone who wants to be the group leader, even if you do not intend to. Because, after all, it is your boss, if not really the whole hierarchy, which decides with consensus. In this situation, prejudices can create animosities between colleagues, and the work climate becomes unhealthy. It is legitimate to have ambitions, but it is also legitimate for the administration to make decisions that seem the fairest to it, such as appointing a person as head of the group.

2.3.2.6. Responsiveness

Don't let others wait too long for you. Answer them as soon as you can.

2.3.2.7. Ways to Using Types of Communication

For each type of communication, you can follow the suggestions below for successful communication.

Verbal:

- Use a strong voice and speak with high confidence.
- Use active listening.
- Use high and clean language (no vulgarities, etc.).

Nonverbal:

- Be calm, positive, respectful, and never offensive or harmful. Choose the right emotions and show empathy. You cannot reveal that you are happy when others are in a situation of suffering.

Written:

- Take time to select your words carefully.
- Use polite formulas in your communications.

Visual:

- The visual way is lucid and easy to understand. But, use it only if it is necessary or valuable.

2.4. Pattern Finding

A pattern is a collection of data that follows a recognizable shape. Finding patterns is a great skill because it's helpful to develop software with a solid architecture. You should train yourself to master it. Here, we provide some points to consider if you want to identify and extract patterns by observing a specific domain or system:

Look Actively for Patterns in a System

- Watch how things happen.
- Identify the elements that compose the system.
- Notice how the different pieces of the system are interacting with each other, or how they are connected to form an asset.
- Consider the cause-and-effect relationships between different parts of the system.
- Collect as much data as you can.
- The patterns will emerge at the end of this process.

Asking Questions
- Identify your elements and see whether or not they belong to the same category or whether they are of the same genre or not. Determine if there are any differences between them.
- Ask different questions to understand the information and the structure of the data you have obtained. Questions should look like why this or that, how or what.
- Determine if you have seen this type of information before or something similar. In this case, use your previous experience and reuse your precedent knowledge/solution if it works.
- Check if the data is complete and whether some parts are missing.
- You are extracting step by step your patterns at the end of the process.

Visualizing Data
When processing data and asking questions, data visualization using graphs, images, and charts is a helpful way to get your results and define your patterns. You can do it manually or use appropriate tools. You will find online many brainstorming tools that you can use for this process.

2.5. Skepticism

The classical definition of skepticism is that a lack of certainty about something will always make you ask questions and seek answers. It will help you enrich your knowledge and develop your understanding and intelligence.

2.6. New Perspective

Create new goals and new projects. Be eager to learn and improve.

2.7. Learn from Mistakes

No one is immune to making mistakes. Learning from our mistakes is part of the process of self-development. One of the nightmares that keep us from following our way toward realizing our dreams is being afraid of failure. Learning from your mistakes is the best way to stop this fear and open the doors to moving forward and achieving your goals.

Take responsibility for your mistake and face the situation with courage. Stop for a moment and objectively analyze the error by finding out the steps that led to this error and what you need to do differently to prevent it from happening again and get it right. To do this, analyze what went wrong by asking yourself questions like:

- What went wrong?

- When did it go wrong?

- Where did it go wrong?

- Why did it go wrong?

Getting feedback from others, especially who have experience in the field, could also help get it right.

Figuring out what happened to bring forth the mistake helps find a way to correct the process. That constitutes new information or new knowledge and enrichment for you and an opportunity for growth. Document the error and the solution if possible to reuse such a solution later if it happens again. The whole experience is a win in self-confidence, and you will not be afraid to fail but dare to move forward to progress for more achievements.

2.8. Innovation

A consensual definition of innovation could be an idea that helps create or produce value. Here are some guidelines to follow to be more innovative.

Dealing with the Unexpected

To be more innovative is to accept to face what is difficult. You must be happy to take on new challenges and be comfortable with uncertainties.

Optimize your Workspace

Make your workspace clean, with enough light in the room, nice (according to your taste), and cozy or at least acceptable to work with. Our surroundings are often an inspiration for us. That's why your workspace should be agreeable to find the flow state to be creative.

Get fresh Air Outside
Once in a while, take a break from your office and walk around the neighborhood, especially if it is the nature. If a park or a wood is close to you, that would be perfect. That will refresh your head and clear your vision to see the problem from different angles. It will help you find solutions that have remained hidden from you. I recognize that I often find answers to my development problems while walking in nature or traveling by train. When you go back to your office, you will be more motivated to work.

Self-reflection and Meditation
Meditation has powerful effects like reducing stress and anxiety or strengthening our focus. It has powerful effects on our creativity by eliminating useless brainstorming and brain chatter and helping us produce top ideas. Additionally, meditation stimulates brain regions involved in creative thinking and problem-solving.

Change your Routine Tasks
There are daily tasks we do very well, and over time they become routine for us. But that prevents us from seeing otherwise. Why do you not stop, think for a moment, and ask yourself whether you can do them differently? Sure, it won't always work, but it will sometimes open new doors to creativity and help you to be innovative.

3. Performance Efficiency and Measurement

A high-performing developer walks into his office, intent on accomplishing as much as he can that day. This directive is central, and it is worth finding a way to measure your progress and how much you perform or learn in a unit of time. You should find a way to evaluate your progress and measure your growth over time during your work as a developer or during your learning process. It helps you to be more effective. We suggest the following steps for measuring your progress:

- Define your main goal.

- Split this goal into small ones.

- Give each goal the percentage (your progress) so that the sum of the percentages of all the sub-goals is 100%. Use your feelings or your knowledge to provide such a percentage assessment.

- Establish a timeline by allocating for each sub-goal, the necessary daily time, weekly, or monthly according to your abilities and your agenda to achieve the sub-goal.

- When the time is up for a sub-goal, spleen your result on a scale of 1-5 (5: very satisfied, 1: very unsatisfied).

- If everything went great and your X percent (your progress) is complete. You can start your next sub-goal in the coming period. If you are unsatisfied, maybe you want to reconsider the same goal to master it.

- When you hit 100% of your overall goal in the exact time you allotted it, that would be good. If not, you need to analyze what went wrong. But don't be so hard on yourself, and stay flexible. We always encounter problems like illness, which prevent us from performing tasks at the right time, and we have to delay them, which is not inevitable. Just accept life as it is and do your best.

Let's take an example and say that your goal is learning Python. Split this goal into small sub-goals like:
goal 1: getting started with python (25%) (5 hours).
goal 2: basics (25%) (5 hours).
goal 3: modules and classes (50%) (10 hours).

For each sub-goal, set your percentage of progress and how many hours per week you need to achieve such a goal. Generally follow your plan, but you can stay flexible. When time is up for a sub-goal, rate your experience on a scale of 1-5 (5: very satisfied, 1: very unsatisfied). If you reach a sub-goal, you can plan your next sub-goal for the next week, for instance. If you are unsatisfied, maybe you want to repeat the same sub-goal to learn it again.

3.1. Master Basics

Understanding the basics of a particular skill is essential to mastering it while focusing on the latest features like programming language features. Otherwise, they will eventually become an obstacle to development. Additionally, understanding the solid fundamentals can often make it easier to get started with new technologies. When you find a concept difficult to learn, never give up. Return to the spacing 'repetition technique' and keep learning it until you master it.

3.2. Practice for Improvement

Programming is a problem-solving exercise. It's about collecting data, understanding the context, and formulating the best solution. An important problem-solving skill would be repeating and recognizing patterns. The more use cases you find, the more context you'll have to tackle each subsequent problem. The more problems you have seen and developed solutions for, the more it gives you a larger pool of knowledge to draw from in the future. In this regard, the three techniques described below are good to follow.

3.2.1. Use Diffuse and Focused Thinking

We have two types of thinking used in solving problems or learning new things.

Concentrated thinking: we concentrate on a certain problem or question and actively try to come to a solution.

Diffuse thinking: we let the idea incubate in a latent or passive mode of thinking. It means we don't actively focus on it, but it stays somewhere in the back of the mind, and we keep looking for solutions or patterns.

We can easily switch between the two ways of thinking. This switch constitutes the problem-solving cycle. According to Agile methods like Scrum, you should take the question of prioritizing into consideration at the first level. This framework aims to release the most valued features to the final user as soon as possible, which is true. But, at the development level, things go a little bit differently. Sometimes you don't have the necessary brainstorming ready to do the task with high-level priority. You want to give yourself some flexibility and wait until the inspiration comes to the rescue. So, let the solution incubates in the back of your mind and use this time to solve other easy problem (front-end problems, for instance), and get relaxed. Do not scream eureka when you get the solution if you are taking a bath! That is the best way to respect deadlines.

3.2.2. Create Side Projects

Side projects are often an indicator of passion and proactivity. They have a positive effect on developers such as:
- Teaching them to add value.
- Urging them to act.
- Helping them improve their focus.

3.2.3. Reading other People's Code: Learning from Others

Analyzing another person's work allows you to step outside the code and try to deconstruct it to learn to think in new ways.

4. Consolidate Knowledge

When learning, you should remember that the main thing is to retain and apply knowledge. We are lucky because computer science is essentially an applied science. The chances of practicing and exercising are almost 100% guaranteed!

5. Teamwork

You should understand and communicate your weaknesses and strengths within your team. To improve your weaknesses, you need to know which team members are mastering such skills and work with them. On another side, you will also help other teammates improve themselves through your strengths.

6. Context

The developer should understand more than the function he is programming. He should understand the software as a whole (big picture). This comprehension of the software context enables skilled developers to make more effective and intelligent problem-solving decisions. Note that this comprehension includes understanding the user's wishes, system boundaries and limitations, and everything related to software.

7. Do not Overdo Copy/Paste Code

It is often an attempt when we find a great piece of code on the web, we paste it into our project, and it works like a wonder! However, if you do that, please do it in a limited way. Test this code and understand it very well. It is good to be inspired by other developers' code. But, it is mostly better when you develop your code.

If you develop it by yourself, you will see a big difference. You will feel that you have more ability to solve problems. Your speed to finding solutions is higher, and your concentration is better. Your pool of knowledge to deal with the overall code base state will be immense. But, if you copy the code all the time, you miss developing such mentioned qualities. You should at least have the basic knowledge to be fast, effective, and advance quickly.

Chapter 3: Software Development and Code Quality

1. Introduction

So far, we've talked about you and how you can learn better. We also talked about the habits and attitudes you should have and embody to be ready to work as a developer. We dig deep into what you should learn in software development to produce high-quality code.

Computing is evolving exponentially, and everyone fights to keep pace with this tremendous progress. Tools used by developers are no exception. Programming languages are becoming more complex, day by day, with new solid, and compact concepts. But on the other hand, many tools are born to help you overcome such complexity. They aid you in learning and adapting yourself quickly. But from the beginning, you should do well by mastering the right concepts.

In this chapter, we will explain why code quality is predominant. We will also explain the principal aspects of the code and the factors to improve them. We will then focus on the main architectural rules that can help you produce high-quality code.

2. Why Code Quality is so Important?

In most cases, a code base grows and evolves since the goals and the functionalities of the corresponding project extend and change over time. Consequently, you should dot your software with characteristics and aspects if you want to maintain and extend it correctly within reasonable periods. Otherwise, its extensibility will be very complex or even impossible to achieve. If deadlines aren't met, customers are unsatisfied because they don't get the features they want.

In most cases, software must be maintained and extended. If some criteria are not respected to ensure the quality of the software code, its quality aspects will be compromised. For example, if the code is not readable, a new developer will invest more time and energy than usual in understanding the code to make changes. Another costly problem you may encounter is technical debt. The latter, also called design debt or code debt, is the further cost of extra work induced by choosing a quick solution for fast delivery instead of a high-quality product that would take longer. That means if you postpone the measures that help increase the quality of code, the development time f your software in the medium and long term will slow down.

A code with high-level quality (readability, extensibility, etc.) is easy to understand and requires low development effort. To achieve such a level of quality, you should apply known code quality aspects by following some rules, such as architectural or programming language rules. The rules will also help reduce problems like complexity. Thus, you can avoid long-term issues like technical debts.

What kind of code issues can you encounter, and what kind of actions are you taking would you take to eliminate them? What are code quality aspects, and what can you do to consolidate them? The solutions are generally a mixture of good architecture based on well-known, long-discussed requirements analysis, technical rules, and various tips and tricks we would like to present in this chapter.

3. Code Quality Aspects

To produce a code of high-level quality, you should respect certain aspects, as we explain in the following sections.

3.1. Reusability

Code reuse is the action of using existing software or part of it (module, function, class, etc.) to build new fragments of code, such as new functions or software. Reusability is a dream for any software developer or company because reusing pieces of projects for others helps reduce their development time and cost.

It is not easy to develop reusable software because its code solves a specific problem. But if you follow certain principles, you can make a big part of your system reusable. Indeed, even for particular issues, several pieces are independent of them. You can develop your code so that some of it solves common problems and is likely to be reused later. You can preserve reusability if you adhere to the upcoming factors, which we will explain in detail later:

- Modularity.
- High/strong cohesion.

- Loose coupling.

- Unit test class/method.

3.2. Readability

A code is readable if you understand it by looking at it without too much effort. Readability is a fantastic feature of the code base because a developer will make its change or extension with less effort and cost. There are a few rules to follow to fulfill this feature. These rules concern the shape (form) of the code or its logical organization (architecture). We quickly mention some of these rules, but we detail them later with examples:

- Follow visual/sighted rules.

- Achieve a good software architecture by following the SOLID principles we present below.

3.3. Extensibility

Extensibility describes the ability of a system to continually allow and accept little or big extensions of its capabilities. This extensibility should be possible without significant changes to its core architecture or existing code base and with the least disruption to customers. Software systems generally allow for growth. Therefore, it is crucial from the start to think about the architecture and code of your software so that it can grow with less effort. The following points can help improve extensibility:

- Modularity.

- Dependency injection.

- Implementing SOLID principles in your application.

3.4. Reliability

Reliability refers to the capability of a system to run without bugs over a specific period. The reliability of a code can be ensured by its availability, fault tolerance, and recoverability. There is a way to measure the reliability of a system, which could be very useful for checking the robustness of your code base and making decisions if the values are not satisfactory. The unit used to measure software availability is called the Mean Time Between Failures (MTBF).

3.4.1. What is MTBF and how to Calculate it?

MTBF (Mean Time Between Failures) of a product is the average of the periods between its disruptions. As this metric is defined to track reliability, the higher MTBF, the more reliable the system. That's why this metric should always be kept high to guarantee system reliability, and that's what most companies do. To calculate MTBF, get the necessary data:

- The period you want to assess (PT), for example, 24 hours, 3 months, or 1 year
- The number of failures that happened in this period (NF)

Divide the period by the number of unexpected failures to get MTBF.

$$MTBF = PT / NF$$

We want to evaluate the reliability of a system for 72 hours. This system failed 3 times (1 hour, 2.5 hours, and 1.5 hours). The time when the system worked without failure was:

$$PT = 72 - (1+2.5+1.5) = 67. \quad MTBF = 67 / 3 = 22.33 \text{ hours}$$

As you have noticed, MTBF focuses only on reliability and does not consider planned downtime reserved for inspection and maintenance but only downtime related to unexpected faults.

This metric is helpful for developers to track the reliability of a system. It is also valuable for customers who purchase the product. They want to be sure they are getting a reliable product that they can use safely. At least two factors can help improve your system's reliability:

- Unit testing.

- Recovering.

3.5. Code Efficiency

Nobody wants to wait a long time to get the expected results from an application. According to an estimation, users drop a website if they are constrained to wait longer than 15 seconds. One of the most common reasons for application slowness is access to external resources such as storage or databases. That's why you need to adopt certain behaviors and follow rules to make your application more efficient, such as:

Caching: storing a part of data that future requests get the data from this caching. Otherwise, you look for the data in the primary storage.

Pooling: let's remember that database connection pooling is an approach which aims keeping database connections open to be reused when needed. Database connections are expensive because they require opening network sessions authenticating, getting checked authorization, etc. These initializing operations take a long time to be executed. That's why you should keep them to a minimum, and here pooling comes to the rescue. Pooling makes it possible to reuse already active connections instead of creating new ones, which helps you saving time.

Database access: restrict your application access to the database, like packing many operations in just one action and storing the data locally in data structures. You can complete your data processing using the programming language. Such processing takes, in general, a shorter time.

Expensive operations: reduce other expensive actions like using strings in the database.

Concurrency: implement concurrent threads or tasks if possible.

3.6. Maintainability

Maintainability is the ability of a software system to be updated, enhanced, or repaired in case of failure. The following recommendations help improve maintainability:

- Compliance with a coding standard like CERT.
- Ensuring readability.
- Reduce complex conditional and nested logic.
- Implementing SOLID Principles.
- Loose coupling.
- Minimization of redundancy.
- Static analysis.

3.7. Security

It is the practice to write code to protect it from any vulnerability or attack that may damage the software that uses it. You can write secure code by respecting the upcoming rules, such as:

- Make your code compliant with the safety coding standards of the programming language you use, such as Java ([7]), C, or C++.
- Use suitable automated tools to detect early vulnerabilities and eliminate them in case of forgetfulness, use of external libraries, etc.

3.8. Documentation

Learn to document and use the best tools you have (private or corporate). For instance, if you followed a process to install an environment, document all the necessary steps and even what kind of troubles you faced and how you solved them. For an eventual subsequent need, write such information down in a simple Word file or use an advanced wiki tool like Confluence to make them available for your coworkers.

3.9. Scalability

Scalability means the ability of your software to fit its growth. If the volume of your database grows, but your system still easily accommodates such extensions without losing performance, you can say that your system is scalable. We distinguish two kinds of scalability, vertical and horizontal.

Vertical scaling is about adding more power to already existing instances. On the other hand, horizontal scaling consists of adding more resources to your systems to share the workload. Increasing the scalability of your system consists of adding more performance and resources.

We will focus, in this section, only on the scalability of web-application and databases. The benefits of scalability are manifold. They keep the application solid and attractive to customers. A scalable application allows:

- Managing weighty workload.

- Keeping response time reasonable.

- Making easier the maintenance of the system.

- Reduce development costs.

3.9.1. Making Web Application and Database more Scalable

There are some points to increase the scalability of your web application or database if you follow them. We summarize these points in the following paragraphs.

Type of Scalability

You must choose the suitable scaling for your use case (application, database, etc.) or combine the two. Vertical scaling is easier but limited and can lead to a resource deficit if your system expands quickly. In this case, you should use horizontal scaling by adding new servers to the available ones to prevent the whole application from crashing on failing.

Distributed Work

Promote distributed work over centralized work. Over time, you will have more and more customers, which means more and more requests that only go to the core. This situation will create bottlenecks or congestion.

Using Caching

Use caching as much as you can. Cache permits storing data to respond quickly to future queries and not grab them again from the database, which is a very costly operation. Caching can therefore improve the scalability of your application.

Using API

Use API services to respond to requests to enhance the scalability of your application. In a REST API, the client and server are separated and independent. When a server cannot serve a client, the request can be redirected to another server. That helps to improve the horizontal scalability of your application. Additionally, many clients connect to API, like mobile applications or websites, which is an opportunity to use API to serve all these cases.

Statelessness

Stateless means the server doesn't need to save anything after a request. Therefore, the servers do not communicate with each other, which makes the whole system horizontally scalable.

3.9.2. Scaling Database

The database of large applications will continue to grow to reach heavy data volume, and it will be a weighty load on the server. In this situation, scaling comes into play. Caching and indexes are used as vertical scaling, and sharding is used as horizontal scaling.

Database Queries Caching

As vertical scaling, caching a database is one of the most known techniques to reduce database load and speed up responding requests. That involves storing the response to a request locally, as in memory on the Webserver, to avoid retrieving this response from the database. That makes sense when the data regarding such a query has not changed and is frequently requested. To determine what data should be cached and for how long, you need to know when the data changed to delete the corresponding cache and recreate a new one.

It is always possible to know when the data has changed because the modifications are made mainly by the code you have programmed or depend on business requirements. An example of the first case would be update operations such as changing a user's address. An example of the second case is a newspaper that changes hourly. You can keep your cache for only one hour to inform your customers on time.

Database Indexes

Database indexing allows vertical scaling of your database by speeding up database read operations. The index is a key defined to help quickly retrieve data from a database table. An index can be created using one or multiple columns of a database table. An index in a database is similar to an index at the end of a book. When you look for a keyword, it gives you the pages where you find it. By using indexes, you can find data in a fast way without having to inspect every row in a table.

Database Sharding

Database sharding is a kind of horizontal scaling that aims to share the load of read and write database operations over multiple nodes (physical shards). Technically, sharding splits rows of a table into multiple tables named partitions. These tables have the same schema and columns as the original table, but each one has different rows. Partitions called logical shards are spread out across separate database nodes.

4. Factors (Quality Attributes) to Improve Code Aspects

We now talk about some important factors from an architecture and design perspective that can help you develop high-quality code that guarantees the code quality aspects described above.

4.1. Visual/Sighted Rules

These rules concern the general formatting of the structure of the code.

- **Descriptive naming:** use descriptive and meaningful names for your code base components (modules, classes, methods, variables, constants, etc.). The names should immediately reflect the functionality of the code element. For example, the name you give to a method should reflect its purpose, i.e. what the method does, not how it does it.

Following global conventions: adhere to the recommended coding standard of a programming language. Since all developers follow the same conventions, the code will be more readable for everyone.

Consistent style and structure: format your code using the same indentations. That makes it easier to understand, which improves its readability.

Make fewer comments: since the names are descriptive, limit writing comments to only necessary ones.

4.2. Modularity

To implement modularity, you must follow a top-down strategy by identifying the components of your system software that are independent but interact with each other. Then, assign a module for each part (main features) and start breaking each module down into pieces by defining classes and functions. Every function should do one thing and do it well.

Modularization reinforces the human being's organizational way of thinking, which aims to manage the complexity of a system by breaking it into small pieces that are understandable, maintainable, and reusable.

Let's define a simple function in JavaScript to perform a specific calculation:

```javascript
var op = (v1, v2, v3) => {
    return v1 * v2 + 2 * v3;
}
```

This function is too specific and has very little chance of being reusable in the future. But, we can refactor this function by extracting reusable operations from it, like 'mul' and 'add':

```javascript
var mul = (v1, v2) => {
    return v1 * v2;
}
var add = (v1, v2) => {
    return v1 * v2;
}
```

These two operations can be used in any other specific or general calculation operation. We can redefine our specific function above as follows:

```javascript
var op = (v1, v2, v3) => {
    return add(mul(v1, v2) + mul(2, v3));
}
```

4.3. High/Strong Cohesion

Cohesion indicates how closely the elements of a piece of code (module, class, method) are related to each other. Within a unit of code, the elements must have a strong relationship to make sense of the functionality of that code. Inside a piece of code, if an element is not firmly linked to others, it must be moved to join another piece of code where it should belong. A unit of code is formed only of elements that have a high cohesion between them and ensure eloquent functionality. It becomes very reusable as an isolated unit of code.

4.4. Loose Coupling

Coupling is the degree of independence between parts of code (module, class, method). Each time this degree is low (loose or weak coupling), the units are more independent. In other words, we can modify one part without affecting the others. That makes these parts very reusable as individual pieces of code. Another advantage of loose coupling is to limit the propagation of errors if they occur in a piece of code. If an exception is thrown in a piece of code, it stays there and does not affect the others. Considering the loose coupling characteristic can allow you to create good reusable software. Implementing some patterns that we present in the following paragraphs can help you preserve the weak coupling.

Dependency injection: this paradigm aims to decouple classes from what they depend on. If an object of a class depends on a service, create an instance of that service and place it as an argument in the constructor, setter methods, or other class methods.

Inversion of Control (IoC): this paradigm means that classes must configure their dependencies from the outside. In other words, objects don't create other objects that they rely on to perform tasks for them. Instead, they get the objects they need from an outside source (for example, an XML configuration file in a Java program).

4.5. Unit Test Class/Method

Unit testing helps you attest that your code works and does what is expected. Writing unit tests for a method, for example, allows you to review the preconditions and expected results and rethink your overall logic that implements this method. You will wonder what an element does here and if it fits or has a strong cohesion with others, etc. Unit testing helps you develop and refine your functions to make them achieve a single clear functionality that passes the test correctly to be reusable later.

4.5.1. Code Coverage

Code coverage is a software testing metric used to provide an overview of the number of lines of code they have been tested. It is used to estimate the quality of your test suite. Therefore, you can know if your test suite contains enough unit tests or if you need to write more to test your code. As a metric, code coverage can be calculated by using the formula:

Code Coverage Percentage = (Number of lines of code executed)/(Total Number of lines of code) * 100%

A high percentage of code coverage increases your test's ability to catch a maximum number of bugs and reduces the likelihood that they will appear later in production.

4.5.2. Code Coverage Criteria

To measure how many lines are covered during a test run, some criteria are defined based on the built-in constructs of the programming languages. We quote here the best known:

Function coverage: how many of all functions have been called during a test run.

Statement coverage: how many of all statements in the code have been executed during a test run.

Branches coverage: how many of all branches of the control structures (like if or loop statements) have been executed during a test run.

Condition coverage: how many of all Boolean expressions have been tested for a true and a false value during a test run.

Line coverage: how many of lines of source code have been tested during a test run.

We will take a closer look at unit testing and code coverage in Java using JUnit in Chapter 6.

4.6. Manual Code Review

A code review is a practice of checking the code of a team member by another team member. It is an evaluation of changes made to the source code before pushing them into the code base. It's a little bit time-consuming, but helpful in some cases. Senior developers should review beginners' code to be sure it's good and doesn't endanger the code base. But, even a senior developer's code should also be reviewed by another team member. Another opinion is always constructive and improves the productivity of a developer.

4.6.1. Best Practices for Code Review

It is good to follow some rules to avoid an exhausting and time-consuming code review. We present here some of them.

Targeted Code Review: code review is usually done after a developer commits their changes and before being merged into the central code base. When you do a code review, you're probably only focusing on new changes. For your review to be effective, it is better to know what you inspect: performance problems, architecture, etc.

Review after build and test: to save time, wait until the pipeline is complete and ideally green to review the code. You won't waste your time inspecting what might be detected by automated tests, for example.

No review code for a long time: you have to do reviews in short sessions because you will get tired and lose your performance and concentration after a while, like an hour.

Give helpful feedback: give feedback in a positive way to your colleagues without hurting them. There is no competition between you and your teammates. It is about collaboration between you to improve the skills and productivity of the team.

4.7. Inheritance over Composition Principle

Inheritance and composition are object-oriented concepts used to set up respectively relationships between classes and objects. You should use these two concepts correctly and wisely because of their advantages and inconveniences, which strongly impact your software architecture. Let's define the two and compare them.

Inheritance is a relationship between classes, where a class extends another one. Inheritance is easy to understand and allows code reuse. It implements the 'is a' relationship.

Composition is a relationship between objects and defines an object (composite) as composed of other objects (components). Composition implements the 'a' relationship and also allows code reuse.

The principle of composition over inheritance (or composite reuse) recommends fostering composition over inheritance for reasons we will discuss below. But that doesn't mean you never use the inheritance concept. The latter is also a powerful and meaningful concept when you respect in your modeling the nature of the real-world system that the software represents. When you intrinsically identify an 'is a' relationship, such as a dog is an animal or a car is a vehicle, then use inheritance between classes. However, if you identify an 'a' relationship like a 'car has a steering wheel', then you should use composition to implement it because a wheel is part of a car.

Preferring composition over inheritance is due to the problems caused by inheritance, such as:

Broken encapsulation: as a subclass inherits from a super-class, the subclass will see all the details of its parent class. That's why the concept of encapsulation is considered broken.

Large hierarchies: if you have a deep inheritance hierarchy, it will be confusing and difficult to see and estimate the impact on sub-classes that planned changes on a super-class will have.

Tightly coupling: any change in the top-level super-class will lead to many changes at the sub-classes level.

On the other hand, the composition has advantages like:

Flexibility: since the component object is injected into its composite object using its interface, it is very flexible to override its implementation.

Loose coupling: objects are independent of each other and modifying one of them has no impact on the other.

Test ability: it is better when you use composition.

To achieve the concept of composition over inheritance, create an interface similar to the super-class, then create an instance of a class implementing that interface and delegate calls to it. Component and composite objects don't need to know each other, which is safer than inheritance. To better explain the concept of composition, let's take an example.

In this example, we define the class 'Vehicle' and its sub-class 'Car'. An object of the class 'Steeringwheel' is part of an object of the 'Car' class. That means 'Steeringwheel' and 'Car' have a composition relationship. To implement such a composition, we create an interface 'ISteeringwheel' and make the class 'Steeringwheel' implement this interface. We add an attribute 'steeringwheel' to the 'Car' class but of type 'Isteeringwheel' (interface) and not of type 'Steeringwheel'

34

(class). The composed object ('steeringwheel') is injected using its interface when instantiating the 'Car' class.

```
public class Vehicle { }
public interface ISteeringwheel { }
public class Steeringwheel implements ISteeringwheel{ }
public class Car extends Vehicle{
    ISteeringwheel steeringwheel;
    public Car(ISteeringwheel steeringwheel) {
        this.steeringwheel = steeringwheel;
    }
}
```

The advantages of using the composition are trivial here. The 'Car' and 'Steeringwheel' classes are independent of each other. Any change in the 'Steeringwheel' class cannot be viewed in the 'Car' class and vice versa. Moreover, it is easy to replace the implementation of an object of the 'Steeringwheel' class with another, which makes it very flexible.

4.8. Design Patterns

A design pattern is a reusable universal solution to a common problem. It is like a pre-made template that you can accommodate to solve repeating design problems in software code. An example of a design pattern is the 'Undo' operation in text editors. The idea of design patterns was known but not in computer science. It has been applied to programming by the authors Erich Gamma, Ralph Johnson, Richard Helm, and John Vlissides in [6]. Many other design patterns have since been developed as programming language-agnostic to solve design problems. When you use them in your code, design patterns become reusable components that save you time during development processes. Design patterns are mature solutions that help you leverage the result of the research and development process for those solutions.

4.8.1. Advantages of Using Design Patterns

Using design patterns takes communication within a team to a high abstract level. When a team member says, in this project we have to use MVC (Model-View-Controller), everyone will understand what it is, and the team will save a lot of meetings to explain it.

Using design patterns allows developers to work at a high level as they work at the abstract block level and are not bothered by details. The details are already well-defined when the design pattern has been built. But please don't force yourself to use design patterns when you don't need them.

4.8.2. Classification of Patterns

We can classify design patterns according to their degree of complexity, level of abstraction, and scale of applicability of the software under design. If we take the scale of applicability as a categorization factor, we get two types: idioms and architectural patterns. While idioms are low-level patterns to tackle implementation-specific situations in a particular programming language, architectural patterns are high-level general and independent of any programming language. All design patterns are classified according to their purpose. Three main patterns are distinguished.

4.8.2.1. Creational Patterns

You can use these patterns to create objects. That helps code reuse and increases flexibility. As examples of these patterns, we find Factory Method and Singleton.

Factory Method

This pattern aims to encapsulate the object creation logic. This pattern helps hide details and reuse code. New objects can be created using a common interface. For example, we create an interface called 'Shape' with one method called 'draw' and two classes named 'Rectangle' and 'Circle' to implement this interface.

```
public interface Shape {
    void draw(Color fillColor);
}

public class Rectangle implements Shape {
    @Override
    public void draw(Color fillColor) {
        System.out.println("Draw Rectangle with Color: "+fillColor);
    }
}

public class Circle implements Shape{
    @Override
    public void draw(Color fillColor) {
        System.out.println("Draw Circle with Color: "+fillColor);
    }
}
```

We now create a class with a 'getShape' factory method to encapsulate the creation of any object of any class implementing 'Shape'.

```
public class ShapeFactory {
    public Shape getShape(String shape) {
```

```
    switch (shape.toLowerCase()) {
        case "rectangle": return new Rectangle();
        case "circle": return new Circle();
        default: return null;
    }
  }
}

public class ShapePatternDemo {
    public static void main(String[] args) {
        ShapeFactory sFactory = new ShapeFactory();
        Shape rect = sFactory.getShape("rectangle");
        rect.draw(Color.red);
        Shape circle = sFactory.getShape("circle");
        circle.draw(Color.green);
    }
}
```

4.8.2.2. Structural Patterns

You can use these patterns to compose objects into larger structures. Some examples of this pattern are Composite, Facade, and Proxy. But, we only explain Composite for the sake of simplicity.

Composite Pattern

The composite pattern allows you to compose objects into a tree structure and then deal with the structure as if it were a single object. The tree structure is made up of objects descending to the common base type. This pattern is composed of:

Component: it is the basic common interface for all objects belonging to the tree. It must be an interface or an abstract class with common methods between composition objects.

Leaf: it implements the component to construct the basic objects of the composition. It does not refer to any other object.

Composite: it implements the component and is composed of sub-elements (leaves or others).

Client: it works with the composition elements through the component interface.

Let's go back to the previous example. The 'Shape' interface is the component in this case. We create concrete classes such as 'Circle' and 'Rectangle' to create the leaf objects of the composite pattern. Based on these blocks ('Rectangle' or 'Circle' instances), we can build our composite that we name 'Graphic' like this:

```java
public class Graphic implements Shape{
    List<Shape> shapes = new ArrayList<>();
    @Override
    public void draw(Color fillColor) {
        for (Shape s: shapes){
            s.draw(fillColor);
        }
    }

    public void add(Shape s){
        this.shapes.add(s);
    }

    public void remove(Shape s){
        shapes.remove(s);
    }

    public void clear(){
        this.shapes.clear();
    }
}
```

Composite also implements the same interface (component) as leaves but contains a collection of leaves (shapes). It also implements other methods to manage this collection, like 'add' to add shapes to the graphic, 'remove' to remove shapes from the graphic, and 'clear' to remove all the shapes from the graphic.

Now let's create a client as a simple class demo. We create some leaves of the component 'Shape': 'rect1', 'rect2', and 'cir' as two rectangles and a circle. Next, we create a composite graphic that we instantiate by adding the defined elements (leaves) and later call its 'draw' method with blue color as an argument.

```java
public class CompositePatternDemo {
    public static void main(String[] args) {
        Shape rect1 = new Rectangle();
        Shape rect2 = new Rectangle();
        Shape cir = new Circle();
        Graphic graphic = new Graphic();
        graphic.add(rect1); graphic.add(rect2); graphic.add(cir);
        graphic.draw(Color.BLUE);
```

```
      }
    }
```

4.8.2.3. Behavioral Patterns

You can use these patterns to manage communication between objects and the flow in a system. An example of this pattern is Observer.

Observer Pattern

This model allows objects called observers to define the subscription to an object they observe (observable) to be notified when an event occurs on this observable or its state changes. We take, as usual, an example in Java. We create a class 'Newscast' extending the 'Observable' class. This class is defined for this pattern, but it is deprecated in newer versions of Java. Remember never to use deprecated classes in your code base, but here we use it, in our example, for educational purposes only.

```java
public class Newscast extends Observable {
  void sendNews() {
    String[] news = {"News 1", "News 2", "News 3"};
    for(String n: news) {
      setChanged();
      notifyObservers(n);
      try {
        Thread.sleep(2000);
      } catch (InterruptedException e) {
        System.out.println("Error Occurred: "+e.getMessage());
      }
    }
  }
}
```

The 'setChanged' function indicates that this Observable object has changed, so we can call the 'notifyObservers' method to notify subscribers to inform them about this change. We define two observers that wait until alerted:

```java
public class Firstnewscastreceiver implements Observer {
  SimpleDateFormat formatter = new SimpleDateFormat("HH:mm:ss");
  @Override
  public void update(Observable o, Object arg) {
    System.out.println(formatter.format(new Date())
        + " > Firstnewscastreceiver received the news: "+arg);
  }
}
```

```java
public class Secondnewscastreceiver implements Observer {
    SimpleDateFormat formatter = new SimpleDateFormat("HH:mm:ss");
    @Override
    public void update(Observable o, Object arg) {
        System.out.println(formatter.format(new Date())
                    + " > Secondnewscastreceiver received the news: "+arg);
    }
}
```

We create an Observer pattern demo class. Next, we create an observable object 'observedNewscast' of the 'Newscast' type, an observer 'receiver1' of the 'Firstnewscastreceiver' class, and 'receiver2' of the 'Secondnewscastreceiver' class. Afterward, 'receiver1' and 'receiver2' will subscribe to 'observedNewscast' to be notified when its state changes. In another words, new information will be sent. The last statement will activate the control flow of the observable:

```java
public class ObserverPatternDemo {
    public static void main(String[] args) {
        Newscast observedNewscast = new Newscast();
        Firstnewscastreceiver receiver1 = new Firstnewscastreceiver();
        Secondnewscastreceiver receiver2 = new Secondnewscastreceiver();
        observedNewscast.addObserver(receiver1);
        observedNewscast.addObserver(receiver2);
        observedNewscast.sendNews();
    }
}
```

The execution of this demo will give us this result:
19:25:20 > Secondnewscastreceiver received the news: News 1
19:25:21 > Firstnewscastreceiver received the news: News 1
19:25:23 > Secondnewscastreceiver received the news: News 2
19:25:23 > Firstnewscastreceiver received the news: News 2
19:25:25 > Secondnewscastreceiver received the news: News 3
19:25:25 > Firstnewscastreceiver received the news: News 3

4.9. SOLID Principles

It is highly recommended to learn and apply SOLID principles for a solid object-oriented architecture. It was Robert C. Martin who introduced, for the first time, these principles in his paper 'Design Principles and Design Patterns' [5]. But, it was Michael

Feathers who gave the acronym SOLID and reworked these principles. The acronym SOLID stands for:

- **S:** Single responsibility Principle

- **O:** Open/closed Principle

- **L:** Liskov Substitution Principle

- **I:** Interface Segregation Principle

- **D:** Dependency Inversion Principle

These principles have changed the way we develop software, and following them helps make our software more readable, flexible, extensible, and maintainable. That is necessary so that our development journey is not a desert crossing because the software will mostly grow and therefore be complex.

4.9.1. Advantages of Using SOLID Principles

The benefits of following these principles are enormous, and we can summarize them in the following points:

- Reduce the complexity of the code.

- Increase readability, extensibility, and maintenance.

- Increase flexibility and reusability.

- Reduce tight coupling.

- Reduce errors for better testability.

We will confirm these benefits after describing each principle in detail in the following sections. Now let's start explaining each principle individually and see how each of these principles helps us build better software and achieve some of the software aspects.

4.9.2. Definition of SOLID Principles

Now let's talk about the SOLID principles one by one. Each principle will be explained using small examples.

4.9.2.1. Single Responsibility Principle (SRP)

A class should have only one responsibility. In other words, only one possible change in the specification of the whole software could affect the class specification.

This principle helps us ensure code quality by preserving some of the code quality features that we mention via the following benefits:

Testability: it is easy to define test cases for a class with a single responsibility.

Lower coupling: as a class encapsulates one functionality, it has few dependencies.

Readability: this principle will ensure that classes are small, well organized, and therefore easy to understand.

Separation of concerns: this principle preserves the concept of separation of concerns by excellence.

Maintainability: the ability to change the software will be very high.

Extensibility: adding new features is very easy.

Example.

Let's create an illustrative 'Calculator' class with some methods we named 'add', 'div', 'isMultipleOf', and 'removeWSpace'. We defined the first three methods for arithmetic operations and followed strong logic to put them together (high coherence). But the fourth removes white spaces from a variable of type string. This example violates the SRP principle because the last method has nothing to do with the first ones. That is just a small example. But, in real systems, the code is much more complex, with several methods and classes. Putting such operations handling strings with those treating numeric values results in the loss of the advantages of the SRP principle above-mentioned.

```
public class Calculator {
    public Calculator() { }
    public static int add(int x, int y) {
        return x + y;
    }
    public static int div(int x, int y) {
        return x / y;
    }
    public static boolean isMultipleOf(int x, int y) {
        if (x % y == 0) {
```

```
        return true;
      } else {
        return false;
      }
    }
    public static String removeWSpace(String inputStr) {
      return inputStr.replaceAll("\\s+","");
    }
  }
}
```

4.9.2.2. Open/Closed Principle

This principle means that software entities like modules, classes, or functions should be open for extension but closed for modification. In this principle, it is allowed to extend the behavior of these entities but denied to change their source code. The goals behind this principle are:

- The existing entities are already well tested, and any modification could lead to the generation of bugs and unexpected behaviors. Do not touch what is already working well. Extend it when you need it instead of modifying it.
- The testers don't need to test the entire flow but only the added parts.
- Maintenance stays easy.
- The principle of single responsibility will be respected.

4.9.2.3. Liskov Substitution Principle (LSP)

This principle stands for that objects in a program should be replaceable by instances of their sub-types without modifying the accuracy of this program.

If S is a sub-type of T, then instances of type T may be replaced with objects of type S.

Let's take an example where 'Car', 'Truck', and 'Van' are sub-classes of the 'Vehicle' class. If each occurrence of an object of the 'Vehicle' class could be replaced by one of its three sub-classes without any impact on the correction of the program, then we can say that this principle is respected in this program.

In other words, this principle guarantees that any one of the sub-classes extends its super-class without altering its behavior. That means you should only put in the parent class properties shared by all sub-classes. Note that this is an extension of the open/closed principle, and it helps you keep your software class hierarchies compliant with the open/closed principle. We will confirm this with the help of an example. Before that, we mention the guidelines to follow to implement this principle:

- New derived classes should only extend the functionalities of parent classes and not replace them.

- Sub-classes should not throw new exceptions because if they do, they are extending functionality they do not have. This functionality should, from the beginning, not be in the super-class because it is not a shared functionality of all sub-classes.

- Clients should not know which sub-type they are calling.

We can summarize the benefits of adhering to the LSP as follows:
- It helps avoid unexpected changes and avoid opening closed classes to make changes.
- Since we don't have unexpected changes, we have a more predictable behavior of the model hierarchy, which will be easier to extend.
- Eliminate many issues when extending for easier maintenance and better testability.
- Loose coupling.

Example.
Let's take a simple example of a class 'Animal' and suggest the following code for it:

```java
public class Animal {
    Double weight;
    public void eat() {
        System.out.println("I can eat");
    }
    public void walk() {
        System.out.println("I can walk");
    }
}
```

Let's take the 'dog' class that can extend the 'Animal' class correctly:

```java
public class Dog extends Animal{
    int noOfLegs;
    public void bark() {
        System.out.println("I can bark");
    }
}
```

But a fish is also an animal, and it cannot walk. To extend this class, you would do it like this:

```java
public class Fish {
    public void walk() {
```

```
      throw new UnsupportedOperationException("Unsupported Operation");
    }
    public void swim() {
      System.out.println("I can swim");
    }
}
```

In this case, you must modify the behavior of the super-class. Since the 'walk' method is not supported by the 'Fish' class, you must throw an exception and violate the Liskov principle. The problem is that walking is not a shared property for all animals. To handle such an issue, you must reopen the class (violating the open/closed principle) and make changes. A good way from the beginning to implement those classes would be:

```
    public class Animal {
      Double weight;
      public void eat() {
        System.out.println("I can eat");
      }
    }
    public class Dog extends Animal{
      int noOfLegs;
      public void walk() {
        System.out.println("I can walk");
      }
      public void bark() {
        System.out.println("I can bark");
      }
    }
    public class Fish {
      public void swim() {
        System.out.println("I can swim");
      }
    }
```

4.9.2.4. Interface Segregation Principle (ISP)

This principle stands for having a preference for several client-specific interfaces rather than one general interface. Create multiple interfaces where each one wraps properties and methods with strong cohesion. Then, you make a class implementing one or multiple interfaces as needed. By creating small interfaces, you should always favor decoupling over coupling and composition over inheritance.

Example.

In this example, we want to implement an 'Employee' class that extends a 'Person' class. For that, we suggest the following code:

```
Interface Person{
    String name;
    String birthdate;
}
```

```
class Employee extends Person{
    String email;
    String phone;
    Double salary;
    Double bonus;
    Double calculateBonus(Double salary, Double coefficient);
    Account account;
}
```

But wait a minute! Not every employee can have a bonus or an account. Temporary employees do not receive, in most cases, a bonus. Indeed, the properties 'bonus', 'account', or the method 'calculateBonus' are not tightly coupled with the other properties and methods. To overcome this problem, you should respect the interface segregation principle, which makes your code more flexible and reusable. It is better to single out the property 'bonus' and the method 'calculateBonus' and encapsulate them in another interface, which we call 'IBonus':

```
Interface IBonus{
    Double bonus;
    Double calculateBonus(Double salary, Double coefficient);
}
```

Let's isolate the 'account' property and wrap it in another interface that we name 'IAccount':

```
class IAccount{
    Account account;
}
```

Now the 'Employee' class will look like that:

```
class Employee extends Person{
    String email;
    String phone;
    Double salary;
}
```

Next, we separate the loosely coupled elements into different classes and interfaces. We now have a lot of flexibility to create classes that implement different features as needed. In our example, we can create classes for employees who only have an account, a bonus, or both. For example, we create a class for employees who have a bonus and an account:

```
class PermanentEmployee extends Employee implements IBonus, IAccount{
    String email;
    String phone;
    Double salary;
}
```

4.9.2.5. Dependency Inversion Principle (DIP)

The official definition of this principle is provided by Robert C. Martin in his book 'Agile Software Development, Principles, Patterns, and Practices':
- High-level modules should not depend on low-level modules. Both should depend on abstractions.
- Abstractions should not depend on details. Details should depend on abstractions.

Why could this be a problem? When high-level modules depend on low-level ones, it means that whenever those low-level modules change, they force the high-level ones to change as well. That is wrong because high-level modules should stay abstract and contain high-level business logic. They should be independent, and the other concrete modules should follow them and not the contrary. This principle aims to reverse this dependency between high-level and low-level components by abstracting the interaction between them.

Let's explain how we can implement this principle. As shown in Figure 1.1 below, class A (high-level class) is referencing class B (low-level class). By using the dependency inversion principle, we will decouple class A from B by adding a new interface A as an abstraction in the middle between them. Classes A and B depend now on interface A, which guarantees the abstraction between A and B. Moreover, the dependency that was from class A to B is reversed to be a dependency between class B and the abstraction (interface A).

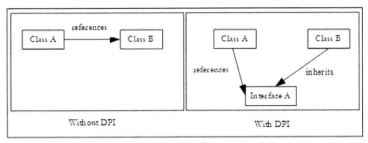

Fig 1.1. Dependency Inversion Principle

What are the advantages of DIP? From the definition, we can notice that using this principle as a programming paradigm helps you implement your software components in a highly decoupled, well-organized, and reusable way.

DIP and Dependency Injection
One way to implement DIP is by using dependency injection. We will experience this in the below example.

Example.
Let's take a simple example of a class implementing a laptop with basic properties in a store:

```
public class Laptop {
    int laptopId;
    String laptopName;
    String laptopDescription;
    double buyPrice;
}
```

Now, suppose we have a shopping cart to buy one or more laptops like this:

```
public class ShoppingCart {
    List<Laptop> laptops;
    public ShoppingCart(List<Laptop> laptops) {
        this.laptops = laptops;
    }
    public void add(Laptop lp) {
        laptops.add(lp);
    }
}
```

The method 'add' will be called each time a customer adds a laptop to their shopping cart. This example violates the dependency inversion principle because it makes the 'ShoppingCart' class dependent on a low-level 'Laptop' class. Also, the store sells other products like printers, mobiles, etc. So, we cannot extend this example to deal with those products. To be DIP compliant, we need to decouple 'ShoppingCart' from 'Laptop' by creating an interface as an abstraction between them. We name this interface 'IProduct':

```
public interface IProduct {
    int productId = 0;
    String productName = null;
    String productDescription = null;
    double buyPrice = 0;
}
```

Any product like a laptop or a printer only needs to implement 'IProduct':

```
public class Laptop implements IProduct{
    //...
}
```

Now a shopping cart can contain any product and depends on the abstraction, which is the 'IProduct' interface:

```
public class ShoppingCart {
    List<IProduct> products;
    public ShoppingCart(List<IProduct> products) {
        this.products = products;
    }
    public void add(IProduct pr) {
        products.add(pr);
    }
    public void remove(IProduct pr) {
        products.remove(pr);
    }
}
```

As promised, we clarify, through this example, the relationship between DIP and dependency injection. As you notice, a parameter passed to the 'ShoppingCart' constructor has the 'IProduct' interface as its type, which is the best way to perform dependency injection. So, as stated above, dependency injection is a way to implement the dependency inversion principle.

4.10. Software Architecture

After describing some detailed concepts that are important to know, such as code quality aspects, code quality attributes, design patterns, and sound principles, it's time to give you an overview of the software architecture and design.

4.10.1. Software Architecture and Design

The architecture illustrates the overall structure of the software. It describes the behavior of the software, its functionalities, and the interaction of its components with each other. There are several common architectural patterns, each suitable for a particular type of system.

Software design is the process of implementing software requirements. It is the abstract solution to the problem. Software design is a phase of the Software Development Life Cycle (SDLC).

4.10.2. Software Architectural Patterns

As we talked about design patterns, we said that architectural patterns are high-level and independent of any programming language. They are predefined architectures. The components of each model are organized in a particular structure to solve a specific problem in software architectures. They are already refined and tested until they reached sufficient maturity.

To develop your software, you should choose an adequate architecture that provides the desired functionality and enforce the code quality aspects. Before that, we present you with the different types of architecture you could apply to your design. There are many architectural patterns, but we focus only on the most popular ones to introduce you to the basics of software architecture.

Layered Pattern

This pattern could implement general information systems like desktop applications or some kinds of web applications like e-commerce ones. These are programs that can be broken down into sub-tasks. Each sub-task is implemented in a layer of a specific level of abstraction. The layers interact with each other. The four common ones are:

- **Presentation layer:** called also UI (User Interface) layer.

- **Application layer:** called also service layer.

- **Business logic layer:** called also domain layer.

- **Data access layer:** called also persistence layer.

Client-Server Pattern

This pattern consists of two main components: client and server. A client sends a request to the server to get a service. When a server receives a request from a client, it processes it and responds by providing an adequate service. Let's note that the server is a permanent listener. An example of this architectural pattern is a search engine. In this pattern, a client writes the keywords of what he wants to search for, and after clicking enter, the request is sent to the server. The latter processes the request and responds with a list of websites where these keywords are found.

Model-View-Controller Pattern

This pattern divides the application into three connected elements:
Model: to hold the data.
View: to show the data to the user.
Controller: to control the interactions between 'Model' and 'View'.

4.10.3. The Software Development Life Cycle (SDLC)

The Software Development Life Cycle (SDLC) is a sequence of phases to produce software. The objectives of SDLC are to reduce production costs as well as development time while increasing the quality of the software code base. As mentioned, SDLC is a structured step-by-step process, each of which provides a detailed blueprint for transforming software from an abstract idea into a valuable, deliverable product.

4.10.3.1. Planning

This phase mainly deals with project and product management, like resource allocation, provisioning, cost estimation, capacity planning, risks related to the project, and project scheduling.

4.10.3.2. Define Requirements

During this phase, the development team will collect requirements from stakeholders involved in the project, such as customers, users, experts, and developers. The development team will logically define the resources needed to complete the project. Requirements will be refined and approved by stakeholders, especially end users. The outcome of this phase is a document called SRS (Software Requirement Specification).

4.10.3.3. Design and Prototyping

The design aims to find a solution to implement the desired requirements and must be the best to ensure the creation of a high-quality product. The software design phase could encompass some activities to generate successively the solution ready to be coded. These activities engender artifacts, and the main ones are:

- **Software requirements specification:** this activity precisely and clearly describes the functional and non-functional requirements of the system. Moreover, it specifies the interaction between the software with its users and other hardware and software systems.

- **High-level design:** the high-level design aims to break down the system into subsystems (modules) and describes the interaction between them.

- **Detailed design:** this level aims to go into detail by defining the structure of each module, as well as the interfaces (signatures) between the different modules.

4.10.3.4. Software Development

In this phase, the developers write the code base. They should be ready with the guidelines (techniques, tools, best practices, etc.) to apply them to produce a code of high quality. We described many of them at the level of this book.

Another activity in this phase could be unit testing. For better code quality, the developer should write and run unit tests to assess that the testable units, like methods in classes, are correct. That is, the actual results are equal to those expected.

4.10.3.5. Testing

In this phase, the quality assurance team tests the developed code to detect issues and assess whether it meets the requirements defined in the early stages.

Many kinds of testing are performed, including functional, integration, and acceptance testing. Note that functional testing validates the software system against the functional specification. Integration testing validates the interaction between different modules. Acceptance testing determines whether the requirements of a specification are met. If a defect is detected, the tester will notify the developers responsible for fixing the problem and updating the software.

You should implement automated tests to ensure that all tests are executed reliably and consistently. For this, continuous integration is the best way to meet this need.

4.10.3.6. Deployment

During this phase, the next version of the software is released to the production environment, and users start using it.

4.10.3.7. Operations and Maintenance

The software is monitored, in this phase, in its production environment to ensure that it functions correctly. If bugs and issues emerge, they will be reported, and the developers will be notified. The new software cycle will start with bug fixes to release a new version.

4.11. Architecture Models

We cannot talk about architecture without mentioning architectural models and the famous: Unified Model Language (UML). Maybe you don't use it later in practice, but UML has a positive impact when you learn it. It helps improve your object-oriented (OO) thinking and modeling. UML has many tools you will find for free online if you want to train yourself. We will introduce you to whet your appetite to learn UML. But, if you want to deepen your knowledge of UML, there are many books and tutorials.

4.11.1. UML

UML is a visual modeling language used to perform object-oriented analysis to generate the design blueprint of software. The purpose of the OO analysis and design process is:

- Identification of objects in a system: objects are real-world entities having data and responsibilities, which are functions performed by objects.

- Identification of the relationships between these objects.

- Creation of a design to implement in a OO language.

As UML is made to design real-time systems, it defines different elements to achieve such goals:

- Building blocks: objects, relationships and diagrams.

- Building blocks connecting the rules.

- Common mechanisms.

Things

They are of four types: structural, behavioral, grouping, and annotational.

Structural things

They define the static element of the model like:

Class: a collection of objects of the same responsibilities.

Interface: a group of operations describing the responsibility of a class.

Collaboration: interaction between elements.

Use case: specific scenario.

Component: physical part of a system.

Node: physical element existing at run time.

Behavioral Things

They describe the dynamic aspect or behavior of a system. There are two things available:

Interaction: messages exchanged between elements for a specific purpose.

State machine: describes the state of objects and how an object changes state after an event occurs.

Grouping Things

They describe how the elements of the UML model are grouped. The package is the only thing defined in this category.

Annotational Things

They are used to capture metadata in the form of comments on other elements of a UML model. A thing called Note is defined here.

Relationship

It is the association or the connection between the elements. Four types of relationships are defined in a UML model:

Dependency: a relationship between two things, where a change in one affects the other.

Association: a connection between two instances of two different model elements.

Generalization: inheritance relationship between classes.

Realization: a relationship between two elements, such that one element describes responsibilities without providing implementation, and the other element implements them. This relationship makes sense in the case of interfaces.

Diagrams

UML diagrams are pictorial mechanisms to illustrate system architecture. UML has several diagrams, each of which can belong to one of three modeling types: structural, behavioral, and architectural.

Structural Modeling
This modeling aims to create a design of the static parts of a system. It includes diagrams relevant to the structure of the system. The most important are:
Classes diagram: describes attributes, operations of a class, and constraints of a system.
Objects diagram: describes an instance of a class diagram.
Statechart diagram: describes the states of a component within a system and how state changes are based on occurrences of internal and external events.
Component diagram: defined to model the physical parts of a system, such as libraries or documents residing in a node.

Behavioral Modeling
This modeling deals with the dynamic aspects of a system. It specifies the interaction between elements inside structural diagrams. Three UML diagrams are behavioral ones:
Activity diagram: describes the sequence of actions in processes to give a view of the behavior of a system.
Interaction diagram: describes the interactions between model elements.
Use case diagram: describes the behavior of a system and captures its requirements.

4.11.2. Architectural Modeling
It is the overview of a system. It includes the structural and behavioral parts of the system.

SDLC Models
A development team can use one of several defined SDLC Models to develop software. Each of these models follows a unique sequence of phases and is suitable for specific types of projects. Since there are several models and it is not a central theme in this book, we present only two to keep you informed and encourage you to learn other models.

Waterfall
In this model, one phase ends before moving on to the next. The advantage of this model lies in clearly defined and well-documented steps. This model is easy to understand and manage. But, its rigidity makes it very difficult to go back to change something in an earlier phase when we are in an advanced stage (for example, testing).

Agile

In this approach, the development team creates an initial version of the software (small version). Then the developers increment the product by adding new features and improving the latest version through iterations. Each iteration is a small step. After each iteration, a new version of the product is released.

This model is designed to put customer needs and satisfaction first. In general, an iteration lasts between one and four weeks. In the scrum framework, an iteration is called a sprint. An advantage of this model is that errors are easily found because the iterations are small. So, the errors could be fixed quickly, and a new version will be released in the next sprint.

This model is responsive to user feedback and very flexible to changing requirements. The rapid deployment of a new version of the software in this model makes it possible to meet business needs. But, this model requires a cross-functional team with a lot of experience and excellent communication skills. Moreover, this model is complex to manage and may require more resources.

4.12. Continuous Integration and Continuous development (CI/CD)

DevOps is a methodology that aims to narrow the gap between the development team that writes the code and the operations team that deploys and manages the software.

Continuous Integration/Continuous Delivery (CI/CD) has the purpose of fully automating software development stages (testing, building, deploying, etc.) for rapid delivery to customers to get their feedback to improve the code in the next increments. The process of automating software development phases in CI/CD is called a pipeline and aims to reduce human errors and speed up the delivery of each new version. A pipeline is triggered after committing new code to execute the ordered steps.

Continuous Integration (CI) is the practice that helps a development team to have a shared code (in a shared repository like Gitlab, Github, or Bitbucket), where each developer can automatically integrate their changes. CI allows developers to work on different features in parallel and provides a consistent project state at any time. For this, developers need to commit their changes using a tool, which is a distributed version control system like Git.

Without CI, developers must communicate and synchronize with each other to incorporate their changes. This kind of work together will be complicated and hard to manage and will grow exponentially as the size of the code and the team grows.

Continuous delivery (CD) starts at the end of continuous integration. It concerns the software deployment phases. CD manages the packaging of the final product to ship it to the end users. Pipeline phases should stay green all the time (without errors). That helps to maintain a consistent process that is always ready to deploy to customers at any time.

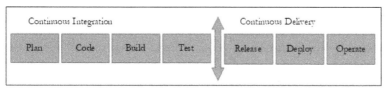

Fig 1.2. CI/CD Pipeline

CI/CD is one of the strongest modern practices which guarantees incremental, fast, and efficient delivery. On the other hand, the product can be continually incremented with small functionalities and will be automatically tested. That makes CI/CD the most efficient and reliable method of finding and fixing bugs. That's why we want to provide some guidelines for best practices of CI/CD.

CI/CD Best Practices
A few points to follow are widely accepted for CI/CD best practices:

Commit early and often: pushing small changes minimizes integration issues with the main code. It helps catch errors early and fix them.

Build only once: don't build an artifact for each stage but only one at the end of the pipeline (all jobs). The building process takes a lot of time, and building only once considerably reduces this time. So, you can continuously push without worrying about the previous version not being completed. Rebuilding at each stage risks introducing inconsistencies.

Keep the builds green: if the build fails, you must repair it immediately to make your software shippable anytime. Always fix bugs early to keep your code consistent and robust.

Maximize automation: automate all tasks you can, such as building, testing, deploying, and monitoring. That will help deliver software frequently and reliably.

Streamline tests: it is good to have tests with high coverage for more reliability, but the process may take a long time to deliver the results. That might irritate the developer, who might try to bypass the process. Therefore, you should find a compromise between performance and test coverage.

Upgrade environment: if your pipelines have been running for a long time, they may get old and not be good enough for code, which keeps growing. Tests they passed before may fail later because the code itself has changed or the requirements have changed. From time to time, check your environment and upgrade it to reflect new code changes.

Unify deploy to production: you are sometimes tempted to skip the process (automated testing, etc.) for rush delivery to a customer. But that's a bad idea. Make your CI/CD the unique way of deployment to find errors and fix them as soon as possible. If you skipped the process because it's too slow, identify the problem of its slowness and fix it.

Monitor CI/CD Metrics: these tools allow you to collect data about your CI/CD pipeline. So, you can use them to monitor it and improve it. For example, if you notice the deployment slowing down over time, you should upgrade it to speed it up.

4.13. Architectural Principles (Logical or Architectural Rules)

These principles define general rules and guidelines to help improve the quality aspects of the code base.

Respecting the separation of concerns principle: split your application into different parts. Each part is dedicated to a separate concern. This principle typically implements a natural human way of thinking. We put together what should belong to each other, and we separate them from other elements, that we think are not similar to them. That increases readability, maintainability, and extensibility.

Splitting code into smaller functions: if you break your code down into small functions, and each one does one thing and does it well, your code will be easy to understand and readable.

Spend more time on design: invest enough time to understand the requirements after a thorough discussion with all involved parties (product managers, testers, stakeholders, etc.) before you start writing code. Also, take enough time to design your solution and think through all the details and situations. That will help you code quickly with fewer errors because you have understood well the task you are programming and have considered all cases. Use test-driven development in your implementation plan.

5. Recommendations for Writing better Code

We now present some recommendations to follow when writing code.

Understanding well the requirements: do not hesitate to ask questions to the product owner or other collaborators to get an excellent overall understanding of future software components. Even when writing the code, feel free to work closely with the product managers, such as asking them questions or confirming with them if you have any doubts about the requirements.

Design the solution: before you start writing code, take some time to think about the goals and design your solution.

Think methodically: structure your thinking in an orderly mode, what is the starting point, what is next, etc.

Do not reinvent the wheel: if you encounter that you have already developed something similar or that it already exists, please reuse such a code or part of it.

Don't repeat yourself (DRY): you should only have a feature implemented once in your application. If you duplicate it in multiple places and later the requirements change and require you to modify some of that functionality, you end up making adaptations in all instances of that functionality implementation. If you make a mistake in any of these cases, your whole system will not be consistent. Thus, it will not behave as expected.

Decomposition: break the problem down into smaller chunks, consider the separation of concerns, and create features for each part. When you write a function and notice that part of that function does something more general (whatever the purpose of the function), extract that piece of code from the function to build another function callable from the main one.

Think abstractly: create a solution that can be as general as possible. For example, if a solution requires the creation of certain classes, first create an abstract class if possible, and then think about its specialization.

Think algorithmically: what is the recipe for implementing this solution? Prepare the ingredients you need to build the code (packages, classes, functions, variables, etc.), follow the step-by-step process to construct your separate components, etc.

Chapter 4: Code Issues and how to Fix Them

1. Introduction

We all want our code to behave from the beginning as expected, but that's too beautiful to be true. The code often does not pass all tests due to issues. However, there are rules and best practices that act as preventive measures to avoid many kinds of problems while coding your software. Furthermore, if it is difficult to avoid them, there are means and tools to detect them in the code and tackle them.

Specific types of these problems are those of security. Security problems lead to high costs if they are not eliminated. To make you aware of the building of secure systems, we strongly advise you to familiarize yourself with the rules and recommendations defined in the standards. These rules do not guarantee the automatic security of your code. But, they help get rid of bad practices that lead to insecure code with vulnerabilities that could be exploited by hackers. Additionally, adhering to secure coding standards will bolster other aspects of higher-quality software, such as reliability, availability, and maintainability. Besides secure coding standards, there are many tools on the market that you can use to analyze your code to find security issues and vulnerabilities to fix them.

We will present, in this chapter, code issues and the possibilities to overcome them.

2. Code Issues

In this section, we talk about the most common code issues you may encounter while developing your software. We will focus on code complexity and security issues.

2.1. Code Complexity

The complexity of a code is intuitively defined by its difficulty to be understood by a developer. It is clear that if your code is very complex, it will be difficult to understand. Moreover, the effort to modify and extend it will increase considerably. Complexity is an impediment you should solve or at least deplete significantly. In software engineering, the concept of complexity has been quantified. So, mechanisms used to measure it have been developed. They can determine when code has high or low complexity, what makes it high, and how to modify your code to make it less complex.

From two different perspectives, namely code understanding and code testing, two corresponding types of complexity are defined: cognitive complexity and cyclomatic complexity. For better code writing, a developer needs to know what the cause of the problem is and what solutions already exist for it.

2.1.1. Cognitive Complexity

Cognitive complexity is a measure of how hard code is to read and understand. Two examples of cognitive complexity are:

- Function with a lot of parameters.

- High nesting levels (many nested loops or many nested if-then).

2.1.2. Cyclomatic Complexity

Cyclomatic complexity is a measure of code difficulty to be tested.

2.2 Security Issues

Many security issues can lead to vulnerabilities in your software. Hackers can exploit these vulnerabilities to attack your code and cause dangerous damage. However, the majority of these flows are known and defined. CERT [5] is one of the secure coding standards which lists these issues and suggests compliant solutions for them. CERT supports three languages that are C, C++, and Java.

We invite you to read the safety rules and recommendations of this standard. Learning the contents of this standard will make you a better C, C++, or Java developer. Since the list is too long, we will only focus on a few examples of issues from this standard. We'll also show you the damages they can cause and how to overcome them.

The foremost issues/attacks you need to deal with mainly come from user-populated inputs (client side like JavaScript), web requests (SQL-Injection, XML-Injection, log injection, regex injection, etc.), data fields input (like HTML/JS), command line input, system variables (System.getProperty("varname") System.getenv("varname")), etc.

As you notice, format strings are easy to exploit by malicious users to cause damage, such as information leaks and denial of service. To avoid injection vulnerabilities, you should sanitize your inputs, normalize them, and validate them before using them in your program. We'll show you how to perform such actions in the following sections.

2.2.1. Examples of Security Issues

In this section, we introduce you to some well-known types of code issues and the problems they could cause if the developer forgot to follow the proper rules to cover up the defect and prevent it from occurring.

3.2.1.1. SQL-Injection

That is the most common problem to be aware of when working with a database. Let's take a Java code example to explain it:

```
public void login(String username, String password) {
    Connection conn = getConnection();
    String sqlQuery = "select * from login_user where username=" +
                            username + " and password =" + password;
    PreparedStatement stmt = conn.prepareStatement(sqlQuery);
    ResultSet rs = stmt.executeQuery();
    if (!rs.next()) {
      //Handle error
    }
    ...
}
```

We assumed that the software user credentials are stored in a table named login_user in the database. The way the request is written opens the door for an attacker to modify it and access what is forbidden to him. The attacker enters a password like this:

' OR '1'='1

and he changes the query to the form:

SELECT * FROM login_user WHERE username='<USERNAME>' AND password='' OR '1'='1'

The consequence of this attack is dangerous and may lead to information leaks or data modification. A better solution to this problem is always to sanitize the inputs (like checking if the username conforms to its rules, for example, no more than eight

62

characters or containing no white spaces), hash the password, and use the parametric query. We apply this solution to our example as follows:

```
public void login(String username, String password) {
    Connection conn = getConnection();
    String pwd = hashPassword(password);
    if ( isValidUsername(username)){
       //Handle error
    }
    String sqlQuery = "select * from login_user where username=? and password=?";
    PreparedStatement stmt = conn.prepareStatement(sqlQuery);
    stmt.setString(1, username);
    stmt.setString(2, pwd);
    ResultSet rs = stmt.executeQuery();
    if (!rs.next()) {
          //Handle error
    }
 ..
}

public boolean isValidUsername(String username) {
    if (username.length() > 8) return false;
    String userWhitespace = username.replaceAll("\\s+","");
    if (userWhitespace .length< username.length) return false;
     ...
}

public void login(String username, String password) {
    Connection connection = getConnection();
    String sqlQuery = "select * from login_user where username=" +
      username + " and password =" + password;
    PreparedStatement stmt = connection.prepareStatement(sqlQuery);
    ResultSet rs = stmt.executeQuery();
    if (!rs.next()) {
      //Handle error
    }
     ...
}
```

2.2.1.2. NULL Pointer Dereference

This issue occurs when you use a nullable object in an expression when a not-nullable object is required. In this case, NullPointerException will be thrown and therefore interrupt the execution of the code, which may lead to a denial of service.

```
public static Integer someFunc(Integer a) {
    if (a.equals(0){
      //...
    }
}
```

If the parameter 'a' is nullable in your application and is not checked before calling this method, it will throw NullPointerException. Check its nullability first and do what is suitable based on the software requirements in this case.

2.2.1.3. Forgotten Entry Points in Production Mode

As known, the main method is useless in the case of web applications. However, developers often create this method temporarily for testing and debugging purposes. But, when this method is left in the code after deployment, an attacker can invoke Main.main() to gain access to the code. So, do not forget to remove this entry point from your code.

```
public class Main {
    public static void main(String[] args) {
      //Do something here
    }
}
```

2.2.1.4. Visibility of Methods

That is another type of security issue. It consists of processing sensitive data in a public or non-final method so that it can be overridden by a malicious method and bypass the security check.

2.2.1.5. XSS Vulnerabilities

These are client-side code injection attacks. XSS attacks are common in some languages like VBScript and ActiveX. They are even frequent in JavaScript. It consists of entering unreliable data into a web application, mainly through a web request. This data can contain a malicious script, which can cause damage if not validated and sanitized.

Consequences of XSS attacks include disclosing a user's session cookie to hijack it and gain control of the account, disclosing end-user files, or installing Trojans. They can lead to redirecting the user to another website or modifying the website content (for example, newspapers).

2.2.2. Security Mechanisms

We introduce you, in this section, to some powerful mechanisms used to solve certain types of security problems. Concepts such as sanitization, validation, normalization ([8]), blacklisting, and whitelisting are widely used to solve security problems based on user inputs.

2.2.2.1. Sanitization

Sanitizing user-entered data is the process of transforming that data to make it safe. A particular sanitization is HTML sanitization which aims to modify the HTML input submitted by a user to make it valid and free from bad data. The new HTML document retains only safe tags. That can help protect against XSS attacks.

2.2.2.2. Validation

Validation consists of checking whether the user-entered data meets some criteria, such as a password must contain at least one number, one capital letter, etc.

Note. The combination of validation and sanitization allows for a powerful mechanism to secure your software.

2.2.2.3. Normalization

Because characters are stored using different encoding schemes such as ISO 8859, ASCII, or UTF-8, some characters may have multiple representations. Two strings with different Unicodes can have the same display, and normalization unifies their notation. Let's take two strings 'str1' and 'str2', as an example and assign them two different Unicode.

```
String str1 = "\u00F1";
String str2 = "\u006E\u0303";
System.out.println("str1:"+str1 + " / str2:"+str2);
System.out.println("str1==str2? "+str1.equals(str2));
```

The renderings of 'str1' and 'str2', and to everyone's surprise, are identical. But, the equality comparison between them returns false, which means they are not the same string:

str1:ñ / str2:ñ

str1==str2? false

These two strings are equal. But they have two different representations of the same character. To solve this security issue, we can use the normalization form concept. The latter transforms a Unicode string into a unique canonical representation and can determine whether two Unicode texts are equivalent.

To normalize Unicode string in Java code, we can use the 'normalize' method of the 'Normalizer' class, which helps us to convert Unicode text into standard normalization forms. Since there are several forms of normalization, we use the so-called NFKC. That is the preferred standard for identifiers to address security issues.

Let's normalize the two strings 'str1' and 'str2' using the normalization method according to the standard NFKC form and display them:

```
str1 = Normalizer.normalize(str1, Form.NFKC);
str2 = Normalizer.normalize(str2, Form.NFKC);
System.out.println("str1:"+str1 + " / str2:"+str2);
System.out.println("str1==str2? "+str1.equals(str2));
```

The two strings are showing identical, and they are equal based on the result returned after running the Java code snippet above:

```
str1:ñ / str2:ñ
str1==str2? true
```

Next, you need to validate your input if you already have a format for it, like a filename or username that shouldn't contain special characters (only - and _). You first validate these strings against an appropriate regular expression and throw an error if they don't follow the defined format.

2.2.2.4. Blacklisting

It defines a list of suspicious or malicious entities that should be blocked. This entity can be a software, a website, or an input such as '<script>' that can invoke an XSS attack. Blacklisting can be an approach that helps you solve security issues.

2.2.2.5. Whitelisting

Whitelisting is simply the opposite approach of blacklisting. It is about creating a list of entities you accept and banning everything else.

3. Solving Code Issues

To deal with code issues, you need mechanisms to find them. Manual code inspection is always a good practice to detect some bugs. But going through thousands or even millions of lines of code to look for issues is a challenge. The good news is that many platforms are developed to help you automatically check your code and discover a large number of types of issues. Moreover, they suggest what to do to fix them quickly. Using these platforms has a payoff in terms of time, cost, and code quality.

3.1. Common Security Issues

We provide, in this section, guidelines for you to follow throughout the development process to ensure that the code is free from common bugs. One of these directives consists of applying the security rules and recommendations as described, for example, for Java (SEI CERT Oracle Coding Standard for Java) or other languages.

Fixing Common Vulnerabilities
To fix common vulnerabilities, it is helpful when you respect some rules like:
- Early on, during the planning and requirements definition stages, you should include secure coding principles to help you consider them when writing and testing your code.
- Your code should have compliance during software development with a coding standard such as CERT.
- Add security checks or safeguards through source code analysis. You can scan the source code for potential vulnerabilities using some tools during the coding process.
- Test as much as possible to detect issues and eliminate them.

3.2. Security Issues: User Input

User input is the principal source of risks that cause code troubles. That's why you should be very careful when dealing with the part of your code where you receive values as inputs.

3.2.1. Common Overall Recommendations
From JavaScript, for example, you need to perform input validations:
1. If your input string is, for example, a date or a number, sanitize before using it, i.e. convert it to its required format (Date, Number, etc.). If it does not satisfy

the format, throw an error like showing a message to the user that their input is not a correct date or number.

2. If it is a string (like a filename or username), you should normalize it before validating it.

3.2.2. Sanitizing User HTML-Input

HTML-Input is a security risk and should be sanitized before using it. This task is usually done on the back-end, like in Java programs. Sanitization can be performed by one of the following actions:

Rejecting content: when bad content is entered and contains <script> as a substring, stop it and show an error. You can implement such a technique using a whitelist or a blacklist.

Escaping content: escaping HTML will force it to be rendered as text. So, an HTML snippet like <h1>Hello <script>badScript()</script> world!</h1>
will be rendered like: <h1>Hello <script>badScript()</script> world!</h1>
The characters < and > are showed as < and > and not parsed as HTML tags.

Cleaning content (filtering content): like removing any script from the input. For instance, you remove the part of the input <script>badScript()</script> from the example above.

Striping content: if possible, you can disallow HTML content. If you reconsider the previous example, you will take only the text: Hello World!

3.2.3. Do Not Trust Client-Side Code

Do not trust any client-side code, such as JavaScript code. For example, don't just disable a button to prevent a user from using it. Any developer familiar with JavaScript can re-enable it again and click on it to run the action linked to the button. So, disabling the button will be for rendering purposes only. But, the real checking should be done at the back-end safe code level (Java or another language), like checking if the action is coming from the logged user with the appropriate rights.

3.2.4. XSS Vulnerabilities

You can use a blacklist approach to disallow <script> in inputs, but you must first detect it by normalizing it (and eventually sanitizing it) and then validating it. Normalization is necessary because, in Unicode, the same string can have several

68

different representations. In the example below, we see a code that validates the input first and then normalizes it. This example considers the <script> tag in the blacklist and aims to detect it to ban it ([4], [5]).

```
String str = "\uFE64" + "script" + "\uFE65";
//Validate the string by checking if it is matching the tag
Pattern pattern = Pattern.compile("[<>]");
Matcher matcher = pattern.matcher(str);
if (matcher.find()) {
    //Tag <script> tag found
    //Handle this situation
} else {
    ..
}

//Normalize the string
str = Normalizer.normalize(str, Form.NFKC);
```

Let's note that \uFE64 is normalized to < and \uFE65 is normalized to > using the NFKC normalization form. This code fails to detect the <script> code, which can go through and cause harm. The correct way to do it is to normalize it to bring it to its unique representation, so the code will detect the (<, >) characters and then check if it is the string you are looking for. The right way to detect your malicious tag is to normalize the code before validating it. The following code will do it successfully:

```
String str = "\uFE64" + "script" + "\uFE65";
str = Normalizer.normalize(str, Form.NFKC);
Pattern pattern = Pattern.compile("[<>]");
Matcher matcher = pattern.matcher(str);
if (matcher.find()) {
    //Tag <script> tag found
    //Handle this situation
} else {
    ..
}
```

3.3.3. Visibility of Methods

There are a few important rules to follow to keep your methods safe:

- When a method deals with sensitive data, it must be declared private or final to prevent it from being overridden by a malicious method, which will bypass the security check.

- Do not increase the visibility of a method. If a method in a class is declared protected and you should override it, don't make it public.

3.3.4. Tools to Detect Vulnerabilities

To fix an issue in your code, you need to know what and where it is. That is possible thanks to the available platforms, such as Static Application Security Testing (SAST). SAST is a collection of technologies designed to analyze, with a high degree of reliability, code to identify security vulnerabilities such as SQL injections, cross-site scripting, and many more. These tools act in real-time while you are coding to detect security vulnerabilities early and prompt you to repair your code to make it compliant. Therefore, they help you improve your coding knowledge at the same time.

3.4. Overcoming Cognitive Complexity and Other Issues

To improve the cognitive complexity of your software, you first need a powerful mechanism to detect it. The good news is that the detection of this problem is automated. Then take advantage of one of the many platforms that will help you find complex functions and many other issues. These platforms are based on the concept of static code analysis, which we define in the next section. SonarLint [15] is one of these platforms, which we will discuss in Chapter 7.

Another thing you can do is learn and follow architectural best practices (more on that later). Also, define packages, classes, and functions well by following the rules of loose coupling and strong cohesion, and reduce the number of nesting levels in the code. For example, if you have a function with many parameters (more than seven, as suggested), you create a class that groups some or all of the parameters to pass the function's arguments as an object of that class.

4. Static Code Analysis

Automatic or manual methods such as compilation and code review are necessary to detect errors and other problems such as vulnerabilities, redundancies, complexities, or compliance with language rules. But, these methods show their limit to find, quickly and with less effort, a large spectrum of issues. That is why a powerful new technique called static code analysis has emerged to strengthen the tools available to identify effectively many more types of anomalies. This method helps detect and fix problems while writing code. The payoff is obvious. As you fix these code issues so early, you significantly reduce project costs and increase the quality of your code.

4.1. Advantages of Static Code Analysis

Static analysis helps improve the overall code quality because it detects many problems and defects in the code from the moment you develop it before you even test it. Static analysis tools act as a guide. They orient you and advise you on what to change, remove, reduce, or add for better code quality. These recommendations are based on some code quality rules that the static analysis tools will explain to you.

Static analysis tools detect security, design, and program flaws, including checking data type and variable function. Even tests are not able to find these issues. We can summarize what these tools afford us:

- Automate code reviews.

- Reduce cyclomatic complexity.

- Improve reliability and security.

- Enforce coding conventions.

- Reusability and extensibility.

Chapter 5: IDEs and Code Quality

1. Introduction

The IDE (Integrated Development Editor) you use to develop your application is the cornerstone of the development process and the quality of your code, thanks to the options it provides you to speed up your coding or analyze your code. Nowadays, we have great IDEs that provide us with tools that make code development and testing an easy and comfortable process.

In this chapter, we will talk about some of the most well-known IDEs. Of course, we will not describe all the actions offered by these IDEs, but we will focus only on what these IDEs offer us as possibilities to improve the quality of our code. It doesn't make sense to give all the details on how to work with menus in IDEs. For this, we suggest you refer to the official documentation, which is abundant and explains each action in detail. But we want you to know all the details of the IDE you are using to write your code. If you skip learning these beautiful actions, you will waste your precious time on repetitive tasks instead of devoting it to the problems solving. All of the commands provided at the level of this book for each IDE presented here are only available on Windows.

2. Presentation of Main used IDEs/Editors

On the market, there are now a large number of IDEs. Most of them are good for comfortable and stress-free code development for some programming languages. As it is not possible to talk about all IDEs, we will focus on the best-known ones as a representative sample: Intellij Idea [9], Visual Studio Code (VSC) [10], and Notepad++ [11]. As mentioned before, our objective is not to describe all the actions provided by these IDEs but rather what they offer the developer to satisfy his needs in terms of code quality, and they do a lot!

3. IntelliJ Idea

It is the favorite IDE of Java and Java-Web developers due to its great productivity-oriented features. When you learn and use all the menus and actions this IDE provides, you will focus only on your work and not waste time on tedious tasks.

3.1. Intellij Idea Overall Features

IntelliJ Idea has many great features that you need to write your code. We mention in this section the most important ones.

Multi-platform
Including Windows, macOS, and Linux.

Several Supported Languages
IntelliJ Idea directly supports languages such as Java or Kotlin due to the ability to be compiled to JVM bytecode. It also supports other languages, such as Python, JavaScript, or SQL, if you install the suitable plugins.

Adding Plugins
IntelliJ Idea supports adding any plugin which is available and is compatible with what you are coding. Press Ctrl+Alt+S to go to settings and search for 'Plugins' and find the plugin you want to install or update.

Ergonomic Design and Customizable UI
This IDE is designed with a great sense of simplicity of actions and comprehension of the code, where almost everything is customizable to meet the needs of any developer. Press Ctrl+Alt+S and search for 'Appearance & Behavior' to change the appearance of the editor (themes, colors, fonts, etc.) according to your flavor.

Shortcuts for Almost every Command
To work quickly and avoid wasting time by writing code, learn and use the most common shortcuts in IntelliJ Idea. You can also create custom shortcuts for your favorite actions. The following table summarizes the standard shortcuts of 'Navigate and Search' in IntelliJ Idea:

Action	Shortcut	Scope
Search	Double Shift	

73

Find a file	Ctrl+Shift+N	Project, Module, etc.
Find a class	Ctrl+N	
Find a symbol	Ctrl+Alt+Shift+N	
Find a declaration	Ctrl+B	
Find last accessed files	Ctrl+E	
Find last edited or viewed code locations	Ctrl+Shift+E	
Find an action	Ctrl+Shift+A	
File structure: overview of its components	Ctrl+F12	
Comment out the selected part of the code	Ctrl+/	

Go to Definition or Where Method is Used

When the mouse pointer is under where a method or variable is used, press Ctrl+Click to jump to the definition of that function or variable. If the mouse pointer is under the definition of a function or variable and you press Ctrl+Click, it will take you to its usage locations.

Select Multiple Lines

If you want to select multiple rows simultaneously, keep pressing Alt+Shift and click in the correct positions of all the rows. Release them and press the button you wish, like delete or move all these rows to the left.

Code Navigation

IntelliJ Idea is designed to find anything in your project in a very short time. You immediately access what you are searching for, such as a class, a method, a word, or a code snippet. As described in the table of shortcuts above, you can type Ctrl+Shift+A to get the popup window shown in Figure 5.1. If you choose the 'Show in Explorer' action, you will get an open explorer with the location of your current opened file in IntelliJ Idea.

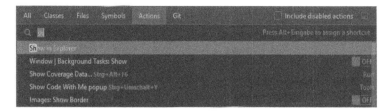

Fig 5.1. Search for an Action in IntelliJ Idea

If you press Ctrl+Shift+F, you can search for each symbol in the selected scope (Project, Module, Directory, or custom Scope), as depicted in Figure 5.2.

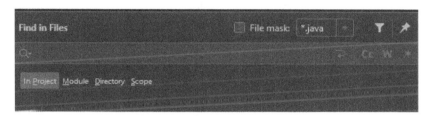

Fig 5.2. Search for a Symbol in IntelliJ Idea

Version Control

Working with version control systems (VCS) is an almost essential process for every project. Required VCS actions are handled in IntelliJ Idea, such as branch management, commit, push, and pull. Most popular version control (Git, Mercurial, Perforce, and Subversion) are built in IntelliJ Idea.

From the main menu, navigate to VCS > Enable Version Control Integration. Select your VCS (for example, Git) and click OK. Your main menu will be changed to have a new GIT menu with all the options you need.

Terminal

Other tools developers like to have are command line in the IDE to perform some actions like running Git commands. IntelliJ Idea integrates this and allows you to do the classic operations, like compiling, deploying, or whatever you can do with the classic cmd.exe or bash.

Build Tools

If your project is Gradle or Maven, IntelliJ Idea provides you with all the necessary functions for automatic tasks such as running tests, building, packaging, and deploying. When you create a Maven project, for example, IntelliJ Idea configures the whole environment to prepare it so that you can concentrate only on your work. It generates the pom.xml file with the basic configuration and all the necessary plugins and repositories.

Unit Testing and Debugger
IntelliJ Idea integrates debugging and testing, which we detail in the next chapter.

3.2. Code Generation

IntelliJ Idea does many repetitive tasks for you, like generating getters, setters, and a constructor without or with fields. IntelliJ Idea is an intelligent IDE. It analyzes your context and only suggests what is possible. For example, if your caret is in a class without attributes, the Generate menu will disable the generation of getters and setters.

At the caret position where you want to generate your code, press Alt+Insert to open a popup window with available constructs, as shown in Figure 5.3. You can right-click and choose Generate... from the context menu.

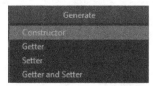

Fig 5.3. Popup for Automatic Code
Generation in IntelliJ Idea

3.3. Code Completion

Who doesn't want a system when he writes the first letters and the system guesses and suggests the remaining text? I am sure that as a developer, you are looking forward to using such a feature, which speeds up your coding process and makes you feel better. It's because you focus on what's more important and not on recurring tasks.

This smart code completion feature is supported by IntelliJ Idea, which even provides multiple code completion techniques. The main actions for code completion are:

1. To configure the code completion, press Ctrl+Alt+S (Settings) and search for 'Editor > General > Code Completion' to find the menu.

2. To activate automatic completion, enable the 'Show suggestions as you type' option in the menu you opened in step one.

3. If you want to enable basic completion, press Ctrl+Space.

4. If you want to enable smart type-matching completion, press Ctrl+Shift+Space.

3.3.1. Basic Completion

Basic completion acts within the visibility scope to help you complete keywords, field names, methods, and classes/interfaces. As you type, IntelliJ Idea analyzes your coding context in the background. It matches your writing with what is accessible at your current cursor position. It gives you suggestions on what your writing intent might be. To enable basic completion, if it is not activated, press Ctrl+Space or from the main menu Code > Code Completion > Basic.

Fig 5.4. Basic Completion in IntelliJ Idea

3.3.2. Type-Matching Completion

This completion only shows you the appropriate types that can be applied to your current context. This completion is useful in cases like initializing variables or writing 'return statements'. To enable type-matching completion, press Ctrl+Alt+Space or from the main menu Code > Code Completion > Type-Matching.

3.3.3. Statement Completion

This code completion helps you write your statement correctly by suggesting missing syntactic elements such as parentheses and semicolons. It speeds up your code entry by taking you each time to the position to write the next statement. Statement completion includes a few types of completions. We explain two of them.

Complete a Method Declaration
First, write the declaration of a method, and after typing the parentheses, press Ctrl+Shift+Enter.

Complete Code Construct
Write a code construct like (if ()), then press Ctrl+Shift+Enter.

3.3.4. Hippie Completion

You can use this code completion to complete words in the open files. Concretely, type the first characters of your word and carry out one of the two following steps according to your need:

1. For matching words before the caret: press Alt+/ or choose Code > Code Completion > Cyclic Expand Word.

2. For matching words after the caret and in other open files, press Alt+Shift+/ or choose Code > Code Completion > Cyclic Expand Word (Backward).

Suggested relevant values will appear, and the corresponding word will be highlighted in the source code.

3.3.5. Postfix Code Completion

This completion helps you attach some abbreviations to the end of the code while keeping writing forward. As depicted in Figure 5.5 (on the left), type your expression ('a' in our example), type a dot, follow it with a postfix abbreviation (if), and press the tab key to get the result on the right in the figure.

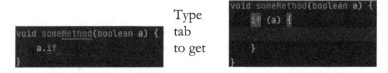

Fig 5.5. Postfix Code Completion in IntelliJ Idea

3.3.6. Live templates

Live templates are hands-on and gain-productivity techniques to increase the speed of writing your code. They help you quickly insert common constructs and parts of statements. Here are the most well-known ones that you should learn:

psfs + enter: to generate public static final String
prsf + enter: to generate private static final
St + enter: to generate String
pvsm + enter: to get the method main
sout + enter: to get System.out.println()
fori + enter: to generate the for-loop
ifn + enter: to generate the if-statement

If you want to see the available live templates, press Ctrl+Alt+S > Editor > Live Templates. On this window, you can edit your programming language templates, modify them, and create new ones.

3.4. Code Refactoring

Refactoring is the process of refining your code without adding new functionality. Renaming a variable, method, or class is an example of refactoring. When you want to change a class name by using code refactoring, IntelliJ Idea will change all the references of this class in different files in the project and keep the consistency of the whole project. No need to waste your time looking for all the references by yourself to rename them at the risk of making mistakes and omissions. Press Ctrl+Alt+Shift+T to get a list of possible refactoring in the current context.

To rename a variable/method/class, put the cursor on the variable, method, or class, and from the main menu Refactor > Rename or Right click > Refactor > Rename.

3.5. Code Inspections

Code inspection is a powerful tool of IntelliJ Idea that helps detect anomalies in your source code by highlighting them with a severity level. The concept of severity differentiates between the most critical and the less important detected problems. IntelliJ Idea will do the whole process on the fly so that your eyes quickly catch the abnormal part of the code and its severity with less effort. IntelliJ Idea has a collection of predefined severity levels and lets you set new ones. Figure 5.6 shows a piece of code in IntelliJ Idea, and below it, a list of issues (warnings in this case). When you select one of them and double-click it (or click F4), you jump to the relevant element in the code.

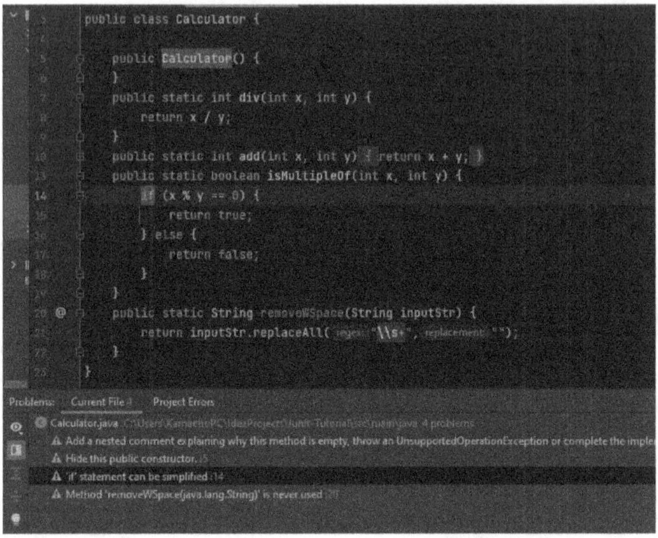

Fig 5.6. Code Inspection in IntelliJ Idea

IntelliJ Idea won't stop here. For each issue, the IDE will make suggestions for a quick fix. You press Alt+Enter or click on the icon 💡 to activate it.

Running all Inspections
To get an overview of all current issues in your project, follow these steps:

1. Select from the main menu Code > Code Cleanup.. You get the window shown in Figure 5.7.

2. You can select the scope of files you want to inspect. You can choose 'Whole project' to scan all files in the project or 'Custom scope' and choose the scope from the drop-down list if you want to analyze only a part of the project. You can add new scopes if you click on ‘‘‘ and then select one of these options.

3. You can change the inspection profile you want to have. Note that the inspection profile is a '.xml' file that contains information about authorized inspections and their options, such as severity settings. You can create a new profile or edit the existing one when you click Configure.

4. Finally, you can launch the analysis of your code or part of it after clicking OK.

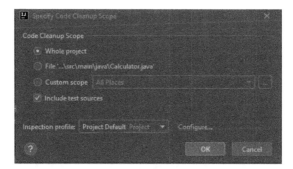

Fig 5.7. Running all Inspections in IntelliJ Idea

Inspection Severity Levels

Severity levels are a unit of measurement indicating how critical your issue is. A set of inspection severity levels is predefined in IntelliJ Idea. We mention the most important ones that you will certainly encounter if you program your code with IntelliJ Idea:

- **Error** 🛈: syntax errors.

- **Warning** ⚠: code that may produce an error (for example, obsolete method).

- **Weak Warning** ⚠: code you can optimize (for example, redundant code).

- **Grammar Error** ✖: grammar mistakes.

- **Typo** ✖: spelling mistakes and typos.

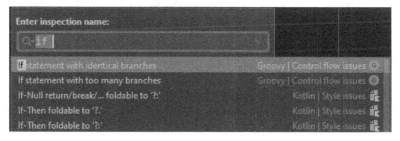

Fig 5.8. Running a Single Inspection in IntelliJ IDEA

Run a Single Inspection

81

Select Code > Analyze Code > Run Inspection by Name if you want to track a specific issue in your project.

Smart Keys

Don't forget to configure your smart keys if not. These are helper tools like adding paired tags or quotes as you type an HTML code (Figure 5.9).

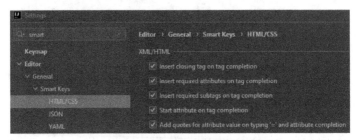

Fig 5.9. Smart Keys in Intellij Idea

Surround Code Fragments

Many standard templates for common source code language-based constructs like if..else or try..catch in Java could be automatically inserted in IntelliJ Idea. To surround a block of code with one of these templates or constructs, select the block (Figure 5.10), click Ctrl+Alt+T (or from the main menu Code > Surround With…) to open the 'Surround With' menu, and select the wanted construct from this list, which is try..catch in this case.

```
public static Integer divInteger(Integer a, Integer b) {
    if (a==null||b==null) return b;
    Integer d = a / b;
    return d;
}
```

Fig 5.10. Java Code before applying 'Surrounded With' in IntelliJ Idea

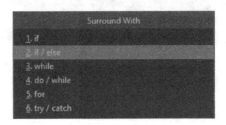

Fig 5.11. 'Surrounded With' Popup in Intellij Idea

```
public static Integer divInteger(Integer a, Integer b) {
    if (a==null||b==null) return b;
    Integer d = null;
    try {
        d = a / b;
    } catch (Exception e) {
        e.printStackTrace();
    }
    return d;
}
```

Fig 5.12. Java Code after applying
'Surrounded With' in IntelliJ Idea

Go to Settings > Editor > File and Code Templates, if you want to edit code templates or create new ones.

4. Visual Studio Code (VS Code)

It's today the star among other IDEs because it's lightweight yet strong. It is cross-platform and available for major operating systems such as Windows, macOS, and Linux. It supports languages such as JavaScript, TypeScript, and Node.js. It also has extensions for other languages, such as C#, Java, or Python. It comprehensively integrates modern tools necessary for continuous development, such as debugging and version control.

Get Started
You can learn VS Code by following its manual you can access through the page Get Started. You get this page from the main menu Help > Get Started. As Figure 5.13 shows, there are walkthroughs to help you discover customizations and fundamentals.

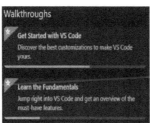

Fig 5.13. Part of Get Started in VS Code

Command Palette

That is the headmost of all VS Code commands you should learn immediately. You will use it several times during each of your programming sessions. It helps you find other available commands based on the current context. To open 'Command Palette', click Ctrl+Shift+P (Figure 5.14).

Fig 5.14. Command Palette in VS Code

Default Keyboard Shortcuts

Using 'Command Palette' to find a command also gives you its default keyboard shortcut (Figure 5.15).

Fig 5.15. Command Palette and Default
Keyboard Shortcuts in VS Code

Customization

You can customize VS Code in many ways. We note the most important ones.

Changing current theme: click Ctrl+K Ctrl+T

Changing current keyboard shortcuts: click Ctrl+K Ctrl+S

Adjusting settings: to access the settings editor, click Ctrl+,

Fig 5.16. Settings in VS Code

You can walk through the settings and modify what you want, like activating Auto Save as depicted in Figure 5.16. In addition to that, VS Code provides another way to change your settings. It is about editing the settings.json file (click Ctrl+Shift+P to get 'Command Palette' and type **Open Settings (JSON)**) and making your wished adjustments. What developers generally like.

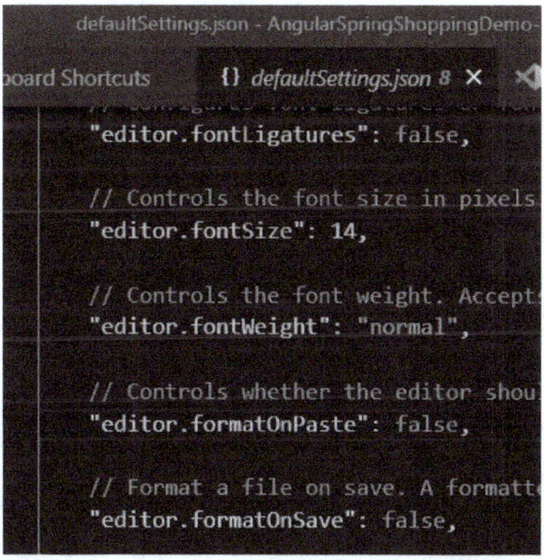

Fig 5.17. Settings file settings.json in VS Code

Find and Install Extensions

Click Ctrl+Shift+X to open the Extensions Editor. You end up in the extension view in Marketplace. You can enter the extension name or plugin you want to install.

Fig 5.18. Find and Add Extension in VS Code

Command Line

You can start VS Code using the Command Line Interface (CLI). To open VS Code in a folder, go there and write the command:

$ code .

You should ensure that the VS Code binary is accessible from there, and the best way is to add it to the environment variables. The 'code' command has several options that allow you to configure some parameters before opening VS Code, such as:

$ code locale=fr

This command allows you to open VS Code in French.

Side by Side

Choose a file in Explorer and click Ctrl+Enter to open it in an alternate view. You can open many views and drag and drop between them. You can switch between the different editors by clicking Ctrl+1, Ctrl+2, etc. It's much more comfortable to work with the 'Side by Side' option if you need, for instance, to compare files.

Fig 5.19. Side by side in VS Code

Multi Cursor Selection

To get multiple cursors in different places, press Alt and click anywhere you want to have an additional cursor. If you want the cursors to have the same horizontal position but different lines, press Ctrl+Alt+Down to move down and Ctrl+Alt+Up to move up.

Column Selection
You can make a selection of several blocks at the same time. Click and hold Shift+Alt, then click inside wherever you want to drag your mouse to make your selection.

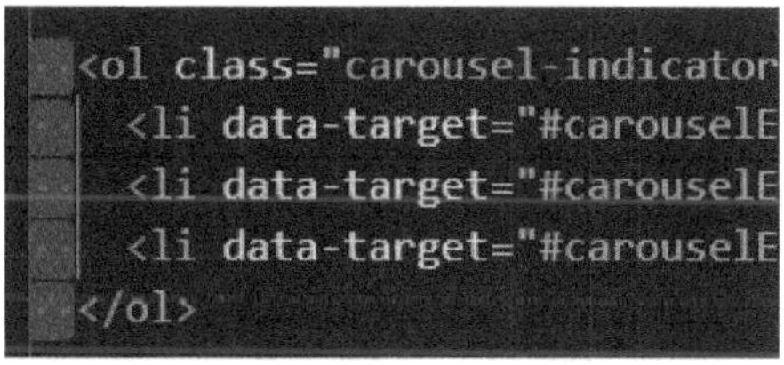

Fig 5.20. Column Selection in VS Code

Transform Text Commands
An interesting function that every developer regularly uses is transforming text into lowercase or uppercase. Call 'Command Palette' and type 'Transform' to enable such a function.

Go to References
Place the cursor on a symbol and type Alt+F12. A window will open to show you where this symbol is referenced.

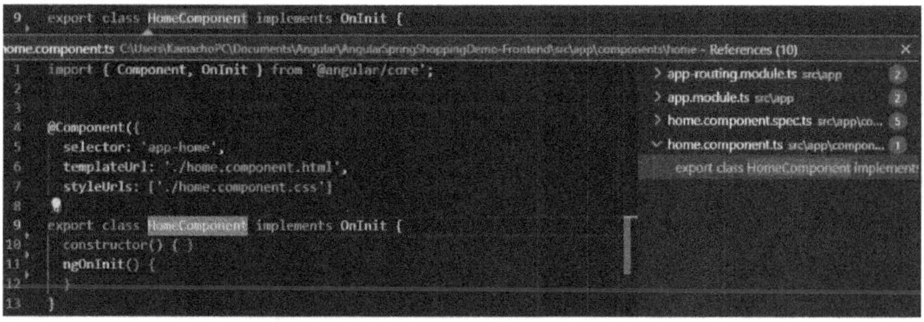

Fig 5.21. Symbol References in in VS Code

You can open view of the references of a specific symbol if you press Shift+Alt+F12 after selecting it.

Go to Definition

Place the cursor on a symbol and press F12 or Ctrl+Click to access its definition. You can see the symbol type when you click Ctrl and hover over it.

Resume of other Shortcuts and Actions

We end this section with a resume of some main shortcuts to quickly perform common actions when programming using VS Code.

Action	Shortcut	Remark
Open recent files	Ctrl+R	
Change programming language	Ctrl+K M	
Go to symbol in file	Ctrl+Shift+O	You can use '@:' to group symbols by kind (constructors, methods, etc.) which can be useful
Go to symbol in workspace	Ctrl+T	
Navigate to a particular line	Ctrl+G	
Undo the position of the cursor	Ctrl+U	
Select current line	Ctrl+L	
Navigate to beginning of file	Ctrl+Home	
Navigate to end of file	Ctrl+End	
Intellisence	Ctrl+Space	To open the suggestions widget.
Format selected code	Ctrl+K Ctrl+F	
Format document	Shift+Alt+F	
Move line up	Alt+Up	
Move line down	Alt+Down	
Go back to previous	Alt+Left	

location		
Rename symbol	Select symbol+F2	

5. Notepad++

Every developer will be happy to use this tool. It is a kind of neutral editor that supports several popular programming languages with code folding and syntax highlighting, which are crucial features for program or text structure. In this editor, you can choose your language and save your newly created file under one of the many extensions available. It may not be enough to use it for a big Java project. However, this might be the right solution for small test applications, such that you want to use the command line to compile, deploy, or run. This editor is handy for scripts, such as Windows batch or SQL scripts, and other file types, such as YAML, LaTex, text, or XML. The list of supported languages and files, which you will find under the 'Language' menu, is shown in Figure 5.22.

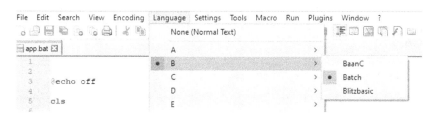

Fig 5.22. Select your Language in Notepad++

It is also a good tool to prepare your use cases, such as for software handling the content of files, which is not uncommon. This tool is handy when you create a new file and don't save it and close Notepad++. The file will remain as it is until you open the editor next time. You can find the official Notepad++ manual on the website [11].

5.1. Customizable UI

Under Settings > Preferences.., you can customize your User Interface (UI) to suit your style and make it comfortable for your eyes.

5.2. Autocompletion

Notepad++ provides auto-completion after typing a word prefix, which helps you save time writing the whole word, especially if it is long. You will also avoid miswriting it. If you write JavaScript code after activating it (Language > J > JavaScript) and type the prefix func, Notepad++ will suggest the word 'function' because it is a keyword in JavaScript.

Function Completion
When you choose a language, you get suggestions for keywords in that language.

Word Completion
If you write a word (variable name, or in a comment, etc.) and you write its initial characters a second time, Notepad++ will suggest it to you again.

5.3. Task Automation with Macros

Notepad++ provides a nice time-saving feature for repetitive actions called macros. While editing a document, you can record the actions you perform. Then, you can later play this recording, and Notepad++ will reproduce the recorded sequence of actions again, one or multiple times.

Example.
An example of a repetitive task is to convert an ordered list of words into a separated list where each word is enclosed in two single quotes.

1. You must learn to think like a macro to use this feature and take advantage of it. Otherwise, it will be like a classic copy/paste.

2. Make sure that (View > Word wrap) is disabled.

3. Write your text as illustrated in Figure 5.23 and place the caret at the start of the first line, just before character 1.

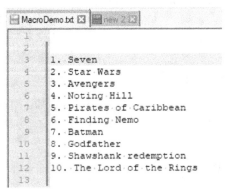

Fig 5.23. Example of Text
for Macros in Notepad++

From the main menu, click Macro > Start Recording.

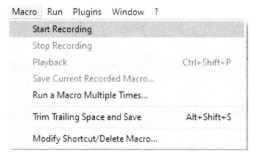

Fig 5.24. Macro Menu in Notepad++

4. Carefully edit the text by following these steps:

- Delete the number 1 and the spaces using CTRL+Delete.

- Add a single quote.

- Move the caret to the end of the line using the End key.

- Add the second single quote and the comma.

- Delete the line break again with CTRL+Delete.

- Stop recording by pressing Macro > Stop Recording (you provided the sequence of actions to the macro).

- Press Macro > Run a Macro Multiple Times to get the window in Figure 5.25. Choose the 'Run until the end of file' option to obtain your wanted list, as depicted below in the same figure.

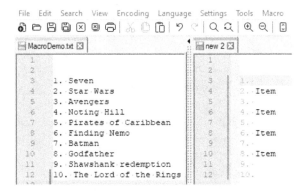

Fig 5.25. Dual View in Notepad++

5.4. Editing

Notepad++ has powerful editing mechanisms that save you a lot of time. Here we present some of them.

Column Mode and Column Editor

To make a selection in column mode, press 'Alt+Mouse dragging' or 'Alt+Shift+Arrow keys'. Column mode allows you to edit the same things in all the column rows, like cut/copy. If you cut or copy in this mode, you will do it for the text rectangle that you can paste elsewhere (in the same document or other) to obtain a rectangle of the same size.

```
1. Seven
2. Star Wars
3. Avengers
4. Noting Hill
5. Pirates of Caribbean
6. Finding Nemo
7. Batman
8. Godfather
9. Shawshank redemption
10. The Lord of the Rings
```

Fig 5.26. Column Mode in Notepad++

In Figure 5.26, you can select the column that contains the ranking numbers, then copy the entire rectangle of selected text to paste it somewhere else instead of writing the ranking numbers one by one again.

Multi-Editing

To enable multi-editing in Notepad++, press Settings > Preferences > Editing > Enable Multi-Editing (Ctrl+Mouse click/selection).

Press Ctrl+click to select different caret positions. Every editing action you perform (cut/copy/paste/delete or write) will be the same in all these multiple locations.

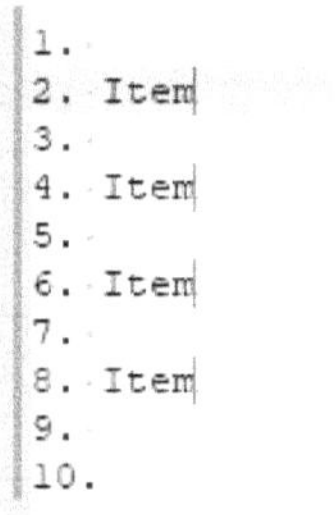

```
1.
2. Item
3.
4. Item
5.
6. Item
7.
8. Item
9.
10.
```

Fig 5.27. Multi-Editing in Notepad++

Dual View (Side by Side)

A dual view is a useful technique for comparing documents. To display a document in the other view, you can press in the main menu View > Move/Clone Current Document > Move to Other View.

You can drag and drop documents between your two views. You can also create two views of the same document by clicking View > Move/Clone Current Document > Clone to Other View.

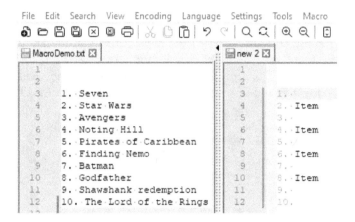

Fig 5.28. Dual View in Notepad++

Edit Menu

This menu includes many useful little features that are good to learn, such as:

Insert: you can insert Date Time in short/long and even custom format.

Convert Case to: to change the case of selected text to UPPERCASE, lowercase, and other mixed-case settings.

6. Choosing IDE for an Application

The criteria for choosing the best editor for a specific application are mentioned by the company which developed the IDE, like PyCharm for Python, Eclipse, or IntelliJ idea for Java or Java-Web. VS Code has built-in support for Typescript, JavaScript, and Node.js but has multiple extensions to be used for other languages such as Python, Java, or C# and other languages.

Chapter 6: Processes and Techniques for Better Code Quality

1. Introduction

Processes such as unit testing or debugging help you analyze your code for issues so you can fix them quickly. They also aid you in improving the performance, efficiency, and overall quality of the code. We want, in this chapter, to focus on unit testing, debugging (back-end and front-end), logging, and other processes and practices like checking for warnings or inspecting code. We will dedicate a section to presenting some third-party tools that can enhance the quality of your code.

2. Unit Test

We talked about testing in Chapter 3 and said it is a powerful practice to improve code quality. As an illustration, we want, in this section, to present the JUnit tool, which is a unit testing framework for the Java programming language. But before that, we briefly introduce some basic unit testing definitions necessary to understand JUnit.

2.1. Testing Types

Two types of tests are defined:

Manual testing: a test is called a manual test if the developer does it manually without using an automated tool. That means the developer will read and inspect his code if it contains errors. This type of test is unreliable and time-consuming.

95

Automated testing: we talk about automated testing if we use automated tools to test our test cases. This type of test is more reliable and very fast. As a software developer, you need to master it and treat it as a development routine.

2.2. JUnit

JUnit is a framework designed for unit testing of Java programs. It is a very powerful tool. That's why we want to give you a brief introduction to it. That might motivate you to invest and learn it if you are a Java developer. Working with JUnit will improve your ability to write code with high quality. We need to create a Java program to start JUnit and run it in IntelliJ idea. Let's create a small program with a single class ('Calculator') to perform some basic operations, as depicted in Figure 6.1. Click Ctrl+Shift+T to create a new class to test the 'Calculator' class and get the menu shown in Figure 6.1. Choose 'Create New Test …' to get the window of Figure 6.2.

Fig 6.1. Calling the Menu to Create New Test

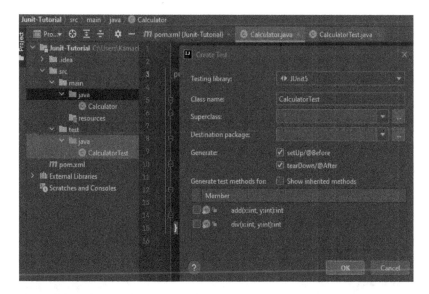

Fig 6.2. Window to Configure and Create New Test Class

The name of the test class should be the name of the class to be tested followed by the word 'Test'. Don't modify it to give it another name, or the compiler won't recognize it.

2.2.1. Test Case
It is a set of actions performed to check if the implementation of a specific functionality meets the software requirements.

2.2.2. Test Suite
It is a collection of test cases to be executed as a block.

2.2.3. JUnit Advantages
As the tests it contains are executed automatically, JUnit has the advantage of helping the developers to obtain immediate feedback on their code. They quickly identify issues and fix them. Thus, they can code faster and increase the quality of their code.

2.2.4. JUnit Functional Aspect
JUnit relies heavily on annotations to identify test methods. These annotations are syntactic metadata added to the Java source code for better structure and readability.

The principal concept of JUnit is an assertion, which compares the expected results with the actual results to tell whether the test passed or not. Test execution is performed by test runners provided by JUnit.

2.2.5. JUnit First Steps

In the 'CalculatorTest' test class, we write our first test method, which we name 'addTest'. It is a common Java method but annotated with the '@Test' annotation which makes test runners execute it as a test. In the 'addTest' method, we declare as a variable an instance of the 'Calculator' class, and we test using 'assertEquals' that the expected result '10' is equal to the actual result returned by the 'add' method of 'Calculator'.

```java
class CalculatorTest {

    @Test
    void addTest(){
        Calculator calculator = new Calculator();
        assertEquals( expected: 10, calculator.add( x: 5, y: 5));
    }
}
```

Fig 6.3. Simple Test in JUnit

Run the test by clicking the green button on the left side. You get the test passed in Figure 6.4.

Fig 6.4. Passed Test in JUnit

2.2.6. Important and Frequently used JUnit Annotations

@Test: annotation over each test method.

@Test(timeout=21): used when we want to test performance.

@RunWith(Parameterized.class): annotation over test class when we want to use parameters.

@BeforeEach: this annotation allows the annotated method to be executed before each test method. Tests often require the creation of similar objects before they can be executed. That's why we use this annotation to initialize these objects.

@AfterEach: this annotation allows the annotated method to be executed after each test method.

@BeforeClass: this annotation allows the execution of the annotated method before the execution of all test methods of a class. This annotation is useful for performing expensive operations once and at first, such as establishing a connection to a database. Note that the method annotated with this annotation must be static.

@AfterClass: the method annotated with this annotation will be invoked after the execution of all test methods of a class.

2.2.7. Unit Test Process
To perform a test, you must complete the following steps:
Arrange: initialize what to test (for example, create an instance).
Act: call the method or function.
Assert: what do you expect by running this test? Compare the actual result with the expected one.

Let's map this process to an example:
1. Initialize what to test, like creating an instance of a class:
Calculator calculator = new Calculator();

2. Call the method to test:
int actualOutput = calculator.square(5);
int expected = 25;

3. What do you expect by running this test?
assertEquals(expectedOutput, actualOutput);

2.2.8. Code Coverage
To perform code coverage, we need to install a tool. We take the simplest, a plugin called 'code coverage with Java'. But you can consider other powerful tools like JaCoCo, which is integrated with IntelliJ idea. We reconsider the 'Calculator' class with three methods:

```java
public class Calculator {
    public Calculator() {}
    public static int add(int x, int y) {
        return x + y;
    }
    public static int div(int x, int y) {
        return x / y;
    }
    public static int mul(int x, int y) {
```

```
        return x * y;
    }
}
```

We write some simple test cases as follows:
```
public class CalculatorTest {
    @Test
    public void addTest() {
        var calculator = new Calculator();
        assertEquals(4, calculator.add(2, 2));
    }
    @Test
    public void divTest() {
        var calculator = new Calculator();
        assertEquals(6, calculator.div(12, 2));
        assertThrows(ArithmeticException.class, () -> {
            calculator.div(12, 0);
        });
    }
    @Test
    public void mullTest() {
        var calculator = new Calculator();
        assertEquals(20, calculator.mul(4, 5));
    }
}
```

We create a test suite to run the above test cases:
```
@RunWith(Suite.class)
@SuiteClasses({
    CalculatorTest.class
})
public class TestSuite {}
```

We run this test suite with the 'Run 'TestSuite' with Coverage' option, which you find in the main menu Run. The result of the execution is depicted in Figure 6.5.

As you note, we have code coverage for class, method, line, and branch. As we wrote no test cases for the 'User' and 'Main' classes, their code coverage values are zero. However, we have covered 100% of the class, methods, and lines of the 'Calculator' class. Since we have no branches, we got 100%.

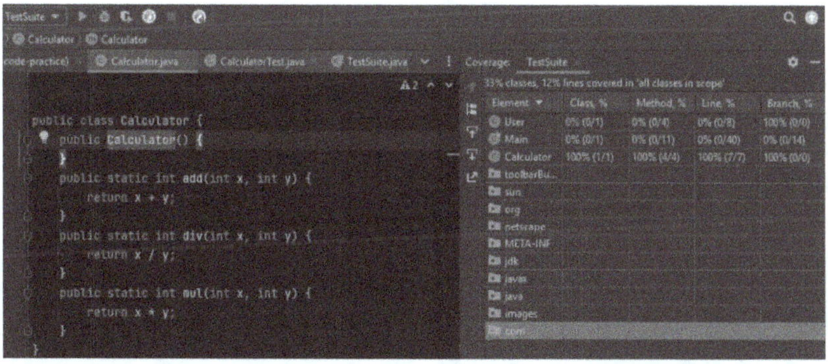

Fig 6.5. Run 'TestSuite' with Coverage by Using JUnit

3. Debugging

You should master debugging tools early because they are powerful in detecting many bugs to clean your code of anomalies and improve its quality. Debugging tools are powerful tools for tracking the state of code to disclose errors if they exist. They allow you to follow the internal workflow of your program step-by-step at run time and to have a detailed overview of the operations of your code line by line. Debugging allows you to stop execution at any statement and monitor the state of the program by inspecting and analyzing the contents of its variables in the current scope. Looking at the values of variables at a certain point permits you to see if the values match those expected at that time and what went wrong to produce an error.

That's why we preferred to add, in this book, a brief introduction to debugging and how to perform its principal operations in IntelliJ Idea by covering a basic debugging scenario for an example Java program. When using such tools, you will feel that you are not in the dark but enlightened throughout the anomaly finding. We hope that after learning the debugging, you will make it a routine process while coding.

3.1. Back-end Debugging Tools

Debugging tools for back-end languages like Java or Python are powerful tools for tracking down design errors by checking the status of your program at any time during execution. Debugging is a simple operation with very few actions. Let's see how to accomplish such an operation using Java debugging in IntelliJ idea.

3.1.1. Java Code Debugging in IntelliJ idea

Check your program and identify the part of the code where you suspect a malfunction to perform a debugging action. First, we need an example to show you how to do it. So let's create a sample program that calculates the average of the arguments entered on the command line, as illustrated in Figure 6.6. Since these arguments are strings, we need a function ('convertArrayToInt(args)') to convert the array of string arguments to an array of integers. This function will call another method ('convertToInt(String arg)'), which will convert each argument to an int. The 'addition(int[] args)' function will return the sum of the elements of the array, and finally, the 'average(int[] args)' function will return the average of these elements.

Fig 6.6. Code Snippet for Debug Purpose

To start in debug mode, click the button surrounded by a white square, as shown in Figure 6.6. But before that, we need to do some run configuration to enter arguments. So, we enter them in the 'Run/Debug Configuration' window, which we get after clicking on Run > Edit Configuration. You can enter the parameters in the field where the series '12 45 8 75' is written, as shown in Figure 6.7. Here we have entered four integers.

Fig 6.7. Run Debug Configurations

We are not ready to start the debug mode yet, because if we start it like that, it will work like run mode until the end. We're missing the mechanism to stop the execution at a particular point. This mechanism is called the breakpoint. A breakpoint is a pause spot to stop program execution at a specific statement. You can set one or multiple breakpoints in different locations.

Hover the mouse over the gutter area of the editor at the line where you want to set a breakpoint and click on the gutter. A red circle will be created to denote the breakpoint, as shown in Figure 6.8, after setting a breakpoint at line 10 of our program. Now run the program in debug mode.

```
8        public static void main(String[] args) {
9           int average = average(convertArrayToInt(args));
10          System.out.println(average);
11      }
```

Fig 6.8. Setting a Breakpoint at the Line 9 of the Program

Program execution will be stopped at the breakpoint, and you will have control over your code. You can observe and analyze the state of your code. You can use the buttons in the white horizontal rectangle of Figure 6.9 to control program execution in debug mode. From left to right: Show Execution Point (Alt+F10), Step Over (F8), Step Into (F7), Force Step Into (Alt+Ctrl+F7), Step Out (Ctrl+F8), Run To Cursor (Alt+F9), Evaluate Expression (Alt+F8).

Fig 6.9. Example of Debug of Java Program

In the white vertical rectangle of Figure 6.9, from top to bottom, four main buttons to control the program execution workflow are defined:

1. to rerun the application in debug mode.
2. to edit the run configuration.
3. to summarize the program: this action will continue program execution until hitting the next breakpoint.
4. to pause the program.
5. to stop and quit the debug mode: to immediately stop the debugger, which marks the end of the execution of the program.

Evaluate Expression.

This operation allows you to closely monitor the value of a variable or expression in your program at any time during its execution. While debugging is in progress, you can open the 'Evaluate Expression' window after clicking the button in the white box, as shown in Figure 6.10. On the right side of Figure 6.10, you see the evaluation expression menu as a popup window. You can enter a valid expression (containing known variables in the current scope) in the expression input and press Enter to see the result.

Fig 6.10. Search for an Action in IntelliJ IDEA

3.2. Front-end Debug Tools

If you're a web developer and only use console.log to debug your code, continue to use it, but only in a limited way. It is time to learn other great tools for reviewing your front-end code (HTML, CSS, and JavaScript). Working with these tools improves the quality of the code base. That's why we wanted to present them in this book and have at least a glimpse of one of the most used debugging tools, namely Chrome DevTools.

To open Chrome DevTools, click the three vertical dots icon in the upper right corner of your screen and select 'Developer tools' from the drop-down list, or type 'Ctrl+Shift+I', or just type 'F12', as depicted in Figure 6.11.

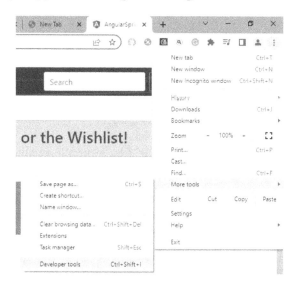

Fig 6.11. Opening Chrome DevTools

As it is difficult to cover all the DevTools items, we will concentrate on a small part to put you in the picture. We intend to show you how good these tools are and to encourage you to use them. For more information on this theme, see the official Chrome DevTools documentation in [14]. The main actions of Chrome DevTools, are shown in Figure 6.12.

Fig 6.12. Main Menu of Chrome DevTools

The first action you take is to dock Chrome DevTools (left, right, top, bottom, or undocked). But probably, many of us prefer the right side (Figure 6.13).

Fig 6.13. Dock DevTools Menu

You see a lot of detail, which means there's a lot of information available to examine your HTML, CSS, and JS code, as shown in Figure 6.13. You can modify it immediately and see what happens without changing your source code. This action will help you reduce programming time. As mentioned, what you modify is not saved, but you can copy to paste it into your source code.

The first useful action is 'Device toolbar' (the button in the black square of Figure 6.14), which allows you to see and adjust the view of the design of your webpage on different devices, from desktops to tablets and mobiles of different sizes. Play around a little bit, so you can test how your website looks on all the different devices without you need an expensive and time-consuming live test on any physical device.

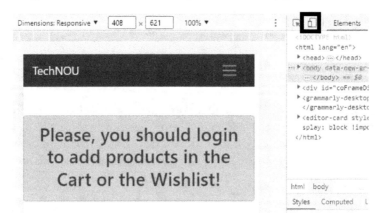

Fig 6.14. Device Toolbar in Chrome DevTools

Close the 'Toggle device toolbar' and click on Elements. Here you can inspect any HTML element. The browser will show the element to you on the design with different colors. It will be marked in blue, but its padding in green, and its margin in orange (Figure 6.15). Click the button in the black box and select any element on the web page itself.

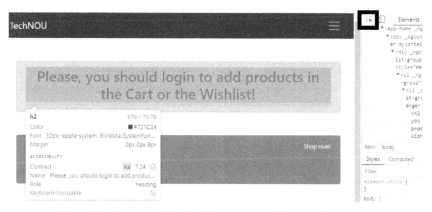

Fig 6.15. Parsing HTML Elements in Chrome DevTools

At the top right, you see the HTML design structure. Open any parent element to inspect the children, and you can switch between the element tree on the right and the design on the left. If you select the element on the design, the browser will show you its HTML code on the tree and vice versa.

The best is yet to come. Under the element tree, you will find a set of properties of each element, like style, events, etc. Let's discover them now together (Figure 6.16).

Styles: it shows which CSS styling and classes are applied to that element. The first component (element.style) is the style applied at the tag level itself. The others are CSS classes that tell you in which line and in which file they are defined. You can click on the file to see its content (source code).

Fig 6.16. Search for an Action in Chrome DevTools

Styles are displayed in the order in which they are applied. The ones displayed at the top are the ones with the highest priority, and they override the others in case of conflict, such as redefining the same property. You see that (element.style) has the highest application order, but (!important) is even higher.

You can toggle any property and see what will happen. The changes will be applied immediately to the design. You can delete inside the element tree or style pane anything you want. You can add a new attribute to the element(id, name, etc.), delete the element itself, or hide it. For example, you can double-click the element text and edit it if you wish, as shown in Figure 6.17.

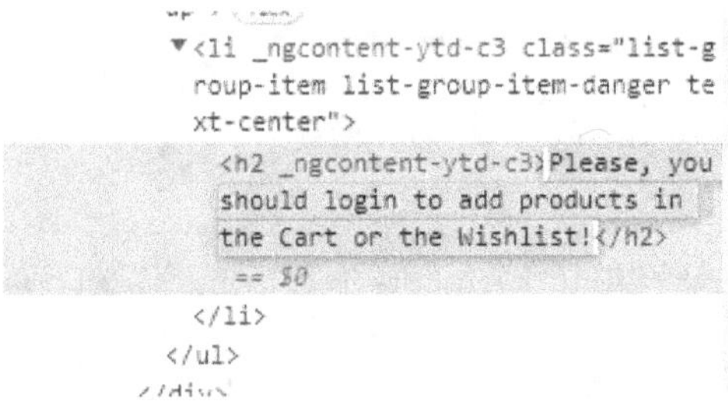

Fig 6.17. Change the Content of an Element in Chrome DevTools

You can toggle any CSS class or add a new one for a specific element. You can force an element to enter a specific state by checking it in the pane, such as a hover state, as shown in Figure 6.18. You can even add new styles to the selected element. We explain the buttons that allow these actions:

Button ':hov': to select a state such as ':hover' and ':visited' in the styles pane.
Button '.cls': to add a new class to the selected element.
Button '+': to add a new style.

You can edit as long as you want until you fix everything and make your adjustments.

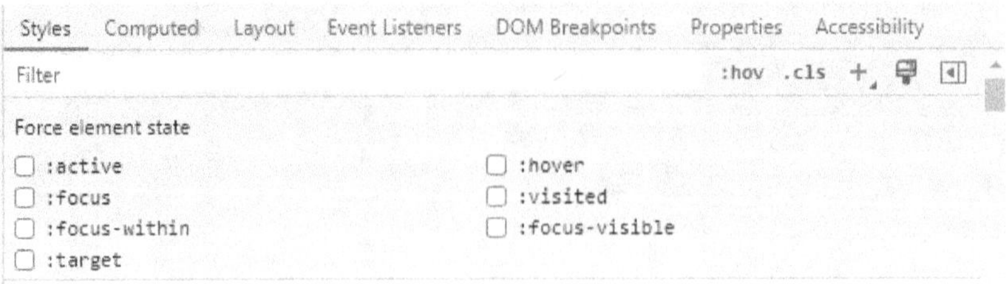

Fig 6.18. Element State in Chrome DevTools

After right-clicking on the item, you get a context menu with different actions available (Figure 6.19). You can use 'copy' to copy an element and paste it into another area, or you can drag and drop it to change its location on the page.

Fig 6.19. Menu to Handle Elements in Chrome DevTools

Computed: in this pane, you check which property is enabled for an element like padding, border, and margin. Additionally, you get the list of all defined properties (font, etc.).

Event Listeners tab: you can check the available and handled events for an element.

Console tab: on the tab console, you can write code using a syntax similar to JavaScript syntax, as shown in Figure 6.20. You can filter what type of console you want to show (error, info, warning, etc.). You can also set settings to filter what you want to get in the console.

Fig 6.20. JavaScript Console and Filtering
Severity Level in Chrome DevTools

Networking tab: the browser shows you all the front-end application files needed to load the page and some details about each file like its status (error or not), its type (HTM... ...oaded. You c... ...ly.

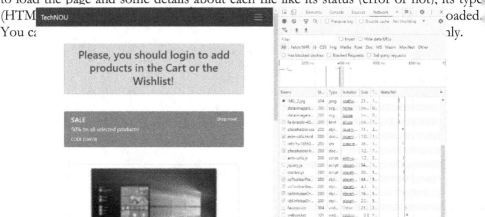

Fig 6.21. Loaded Files in Network

Tab in Chrome DevTools

That's not all. If you click on one of these files, you will see a lot of information about it. This information is useful for detecting problems, especially concerning files that request the server (Figure 6.22). You can check the request details to verify whether it is successful, what kind of response you get, like JSON array or HTML

110

(response tab), and examine whether it is the expected one. At what point in the program was your function called (initiator tab), and how long did the request and response take (timing tab)? The preview tab is used to create a view of files like images.

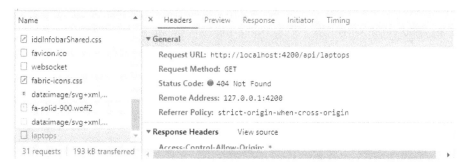

Fig 6.22. Information about a File

in Networking Tab in Chrome DevTools

Application tab: you consult this tab if your application deals with cookies, sessions, or local storage. You can check what is inside these cookies or storage and clear them.

Performance tab: Chrome DevTools allows you to analyze the performance of your page at run time. Let's see how it works. Click the Record button to capture performance metrics (or profiles) as the page runs (Figure 6.23).

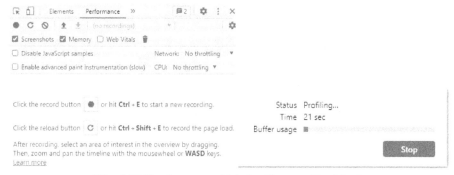

Fig 6.23 Performance Tab in Chrome DevTools

You can stop recording whenever you want, let's say 5 seconds. After that, Chrome DevTools will display the results in the Performance panel during these 5 seconds, as shown in Figure 6.24. You can analyze how good or bad your page performance was to find out the causes. For example, you can see how long a part of the page took to load. That is useful for determining which program piece is taking too long to run.

You have a few settings above (Figure 6.24) that you can change for further testing. You can change the CPU conditions by slowing it down and simulating how your website works on a slower device.

Fig 6.24. Performance Data in Chrome DevTools

Debugging: you can start debugging your code if you open a source file you want to debug. Choose the line to set your breakpoint, click on the line number (on number 1 in our example, as shown in Figure 6.25), and reload the page. Debug buttons are shown in the black rectangle in Figure 6.25.

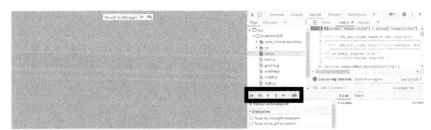

Fig 6.25. Switching in Debug Mode in Chrome DevTools

We zoomed these buttons in Figure 6.26. You can use these buttons to step through your code and control the program execution workflow.

Fig 6.26. Debugging Menu in Chrome DevTools

112

From left to right, the buttons allow the following actions:

- Resume script execution (F8 or Ctrl+\).

- Step over next function call (F10 or Ctrl+').

- Step into next function call (F11 or Ctrl+;).

- Step out of current function (Shift+F11 or Ctrl+Shift+;).

- Step (F9).

- Deactivate breakpoints (Ctrl+F8).

The small pane in Figure 6.27 indicates that the state of the code is paused in the debugger. Two buttons are available inside this pane, the 'Resume script execution' and the 'Step over next function call' one.

Fig 6.27. Debug Pane in Chrome DevTools

4. Logging

To better monitor your application to quickly find flaws or understand what happened while your application is in use, a good way is to keep track of everything that happened during the execution of the application. It's called logging, and it's a powerful practice when you're testing your code or in production. Investing in logging will help you increase the quality of your code. In this section, we want to present some points to follow and consider for successful logging.

Logging Library

Choose the log library suitable for the programming languages you code with. Languages like Java have powerful logging libraries like Log4j.

Selecting Appenders

Appendices specify where your log events will be written. Appenders are responsible for formatting these events and sending them to an output. The best-known appenders are console and file. You should select appenders that meet your application requirements and allow you to debug your code during development or when it runs in production.

Severity Levels

It is necessary to consider security levels and use them correctly. Writing logging distinguishing between errors, warnings, info, and other security levels, is informative, easy to read, and powerful for identifying what went wrong on the fly. Moreover, this categorization allows you to easily search and filter your logged data according to severity levels. Imagine if they were all logged at one severity level, like info!

Optimizing Log Data

The log you write should be clear and understandable as it will be read frequently by others (for example, teammates) to find and solve problems. Even if it is your log, it can be difficult to understand the corresponding code, in case you developed it a long time ago and forgot it. But clear, precise, and meaningful logging is great for getting a quick picture to solve problems, regardless of who is doing the job. Avoid being too abstract and note precisely the cause of the problem that may arise. Record the error code and message if it contains such data.

Add Contextual Information

You should include in your logging metadata, such as the class and method where the problem occurs, if the used library does not allow their automatic addition. Thus, you can know where the issue has taken place.

Consistency of Log Structure

Keep the same structure and order when writing your log messages. In other words, if your log message contains data such as class name, method name, error code, and error message, then each log message must contain these same data in the same order and formatted in the same way. Following the same standard for formatting log messages makes your log easier to understand.

Performance Effect

Logging events are statements like any other. They can contain calls to methods that can be slow and expensive. So, you should be aware of the performance issue and refine your logging to stay efficient.

Log Exceptions

Print the contents of your exceptions accurately. If they are not displayed, you may not recognize the cause of the problems that disrupted the execution of your application.

Hiding Sensitive Information

One important thing, you should hide sensitive information such as passwords, credit card numbers, access tokens, etc. You must not show these data in your logging.

5. Warnings

As we talked about code inspection in IntelliJ Idea in Chapter 5, we mentioned severity level to differentiate between the seriousness of issues. One specific severity level is warnings. Warnings are powerful mechanisms for improving code quality that you should always consider when you write code.

Fig 6.28. Warnings in Java Code in IntelliJ Idea

The first warning (line 11) draws your attention to using a better logger than system.out for logging, as shown in Figure 6.28. The second warning (line 14) incites you to replace the map parameter (lambda) with a method reference like this:

List<Integer> argsalist =

Arrays.*stream*(args).map(Main::*convertToInt*).collect(Collectors.*toList*());

Warnings are undoubtedly strong mechanisms to improve code quality.

6. Code Analysis

As mentioned in Chapter 5, you can start code analysis from the main menu by clicking Code > Inspect Code.. to get the popup in Figure 6.29. Configure the scope of your analysis and click OK.

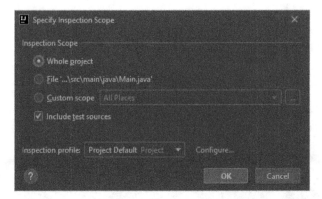

Fig 6.29. Configuration of Code Analysis in IntelliJ Idea

Some issues will be detected, and suggestions will be provided for you to fix and improve the quality of your code. For example, if we click on the button in the white box in Figure 6.30, the suggested solution will be carried out automatically inside the code.

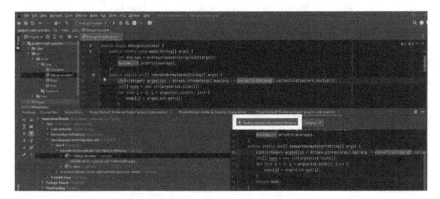

Fig 6.30. Suggestions to Improve Code
after Code Analysis in IntelliJ Idea

7. Third Party Tools and Plugins

You will also find good free and easy-to-use tools that help you to boost your productivity. They aid you in detecting different issues in your code, speeding up writing your code, or automating recurring tasks. We present some of them in this section.

7.1. Tabnine

Tabnine [14] is an AI assistant anticipating coding needs to provide code completions. It supports many programming languages, including Java, Python, and JavaScript. Tabnine is a plugin to install from the marketplace in IntelliJ Idea, for example.

7.2. SonarLint

SonarLint [15] is a SonarQube plugin designed for static code analysis. It can be installed from the marketplace. It works in the background and helps developers address quality and security issues while coding. Among what this tool can suggest for improving the code:

- Delete unnecessary code.

- Detect duplicate code.

- Review the complexity of a function, such as having too many parameters, etc.

- Suggest changing a piece of code like 'for (let i=0; i<list.length;i++)' to simple 'for of': 'for (let x of list)' in JQuery.

This tool supports many programming languages (Java, Python, JQuery, etc.). The example illustrated in Figure 6.31 shows how SonarLint is used when coding with the Java language.

Fig 6.31. SonarLint Static Analysis Examples
for Java Program in IntelliJ Idea

What is also good with this tool is to find on the right side details of the rule that has been broken. The explanation will be followed by an example allowing you to know more about the topic (the problem and the suggested solution).

7.3. Lombock

It's a small Java library and a great tool for significantly minimizing boilerplate code. It saves time, effort, and even space to increase the readability of the code.

Instead of generating basic operations like getter or setter in a class by yourself, this tool enables you to add them as annotations, as shown in Figure 6.32. When you add the @Getter and @Setter annotations to a class, the class will implicitly join a getter and a setter to each property.

Fig 6.32. Lombock Getter and Setter Annotations

118

Chapter 7: Programming Tips for Better Code Quality

1. Introduction

In this chapter, we want to end this book with some programming tips for better clean code. We want you to be aware of some details that you may forget. But they can make your code shorter, more readable, understandable, robust, and efficient. Your tagline should always be: high-level code is less writing and more coding. We focus for simplicity reasons only on Java and JQuery programming languages.

2. Programming Patterns

We present, in this section, some simple rules to follow when writing code. They make it possible to produce clean code and save a colossal amount of time. Therefore, you can perform more tasks and focus more on business logic.

2.1. Consistent Name Scheme

You must always give the most appropriate names to your variables, functions, files, etc. These names should specify the purpose of the defined elements. As their names reflected their roles, it is easy to memorize them and find them using the search tools of some IDEs, such as IntelliJ Idea or VS Code, as explained in Chapter 5.

For example, instead of declaring the following variable and an unnecessary comment like this:

//this is the username variable
var us = "Mark";

You can define the variable with a very descriptive name like this:

var username = "Mark";

You can use comments for TODO purposes to remind yourself or your teammates to finish, for example, an unfinished job (Figure 7.1).

Fig 7.1. TODO in Java Program in IntelliJ Idea

2.2. Magic Strings/Numbers

You should avoid using constant strings or numbers directly inside a statement. Let's take an example:

```
if (age > 21){
    //Do something
}
```

In this example, you cannot know the context of the number 21. You should better declare it as a constant with an appropriate name like this:

```
const LEGAL_DRINKING_AGE = 21;
if (age > LEGAL_DRINKING_AGE){
    //Do something
}
```

2.3. Making Comments only as Necessary

Comments are very good for code readability. But, they should only be defined when the part of the code is not self-explanatory. For example, when writing a declaration like this:

```
var username = "Mark";
```

This statement needs no comment. It is already self-explanatory.

2.4. Formatting and Coding Style

Coding style and formatting affect the readability and maintainability of your code. Adding proper white spaces, indentation, and line breaks to the code makes it easy to read and understand. Figure 7.2 shows a structured code snippet written in Java.

```java
public byte[] changeTextFileCaseAction(InputStream is, String action) {
    BufferedReader br = null;
    StringBuilder str = new StringBuilder();
    try {
        Reader reader = new InputStreamReader(is);
        br = new BufferedReader(reader);
        String strLine;
        while ((strLine = br.readLine()) != null) {
            String result = changeCaseAction(strLine, action);
            str.append(result+"\n");
        }
    } catch (Exception e) {
        e.printStackTrace();
    } finally {
        try {
            if (br != null)
                br.close();
        } catch (IOException e) {
            e.printStackTrace();
        }
    }
    return str.toString().getBytes(Charset.forName("UTF-8"));
}
```

Fig 7.2. Structured Snippet of Code written in Java in IntelliJ Idea

2.5. Learning Global Coding Convention

Respecting code conventions is very important for developers. First and foremost, software code is often written and maintained by different developers and not just one. Code convention, in this case, is standardization among developers to help them quickly understand what others have done. On another side, it decreases cognitive complexity for better code readability. If you take the Java language, for example, its specification recommends that Java modifiers should be declared in the following order:

For fields: @Annotation public protected private static final transient volatile

For methods: @Annotation public protected private abstract static final synchronized native strictfp

121

Let's declare a class with some variables, as shown in Figure 7.3. The declaration of the variable 'x' follows standard Java coding, but the declaration of the variable 'y' does not. That has no technical impact on the program because it will run normally and return the same result as if the normalization of the coding were respected. The problem is the reduced code readability because most developers are used to following the standard order.

```java
public class Main {

    public static final int x = 10;
    private final static int y = 12;
    public static void main(String[] args){
        int z = x + y;
        System.out.println(z);
    }
}
```

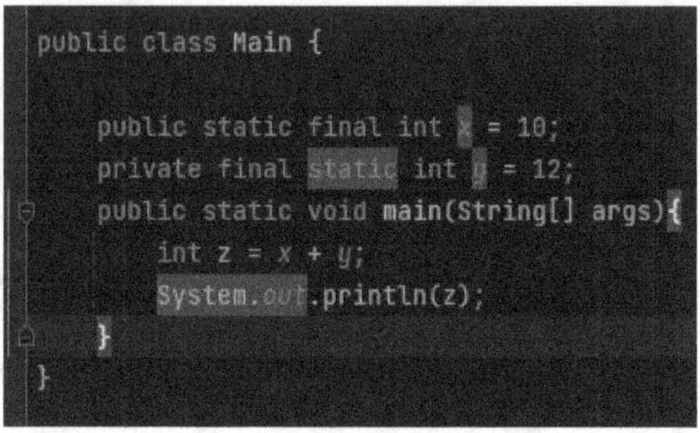

Fig 7.3. Example Respecting Java Standard
Coding in Java in IntelliJ Idea

2.6. Use Underlines in Lengthy Numeric

A useful feature of Java for Numeric consists of using underlines in long numbers. This feature makes your code more understandable and well-structured. So, instead of writing:
int number = 457895412;

You can separate the lengthy number using underscores like this:
int number = 457_895_412;

2.7. Delete Poltergeist Code

Many developers think it's good to keep certain parts of code commented out, so they can use them later. But, these code snippets will quickly become noisy and confusing. We recommend keeping them in an extra file or a branch if you're using the Git tool and removing them from your main working code to keep it always clean.

3. Quick Typing and Shortcuts

If you feel that you are not typing fast enough on the keyboard while writing code, take a class or learn it on your own to improve your typing speed. That will undoubtedly help you save time and have more time to improve your business logic or perform more tasks. Another trick to speed up your typing is to take advantage of features provided by IDEs, such as turning on auto-save or learning common keyboard shortcuts. We already had an overview of using shortcuts in three different IDEs in Chapter 5: IntelliJ Idea, VS Code, and Notepad++.

4. Learning Tips (Best Practices)

When using a programming language to code, you should always be aware of following the best practices or tips specific to that programming language to code better.

For example, suppose you want to store unique values in Java. If you use a list, you should do extra work after any operation to check that values are not repeated. However, if you use a set to store your data, that will automatically ensure that no value will be repeated.

4.2. Best Practices in Java

In this section, we'll share with you some Java-specific techniques to improve the quality of your code.

Statement 'switch-case' instead of 'if-then-else'

It is possible to replace 'if-then-else' with 'switch-case' if it is a simple comparison of variables or multi-valued expressions and execute the appropriate code if there is a match. If you have an 'if-then-else' statement that you can replace with the 'switch-case' statement, it's usually best to use the latter due to its compact form and clarity. Remember that the 'switch-case' expression can be of type byte, char, or int. Since Java 7, it can also be of enumeration, string, or wrapper class type.

Let's take an example to compare between 'if-then-else' and 'switch-case'. For that, we define a simple enumeration type:

```java
public enum Day {
    SUNDAY, MONDAY, TUESDAY, WEDNESDAY,
    THURSDAY, FRIDAY, SATURDAY
}
if (day.equals(Day.MONDAY)){
    System.out.println("Oh, Work, Work, Work...");
} else if (day.equals(Day.FRIDAY)){
```

```
    System.out.println("Thank you God, it is Friday!");
} else if (day.equals(Day.SATURDAY)||day.equals(Day.SUNDAY)){
    System.out.println("Relax and enjoy your Weekend!");
} else {
    System.out.println("Work, what else?");
}
```

The equivalent 'switch-case' is straightforward and easily readable. It is simpler to understand the purpose of this statement with minimal effort.

```
switch (day) {
    case MONDAY: System.out.println("Oh, Work, Work, Work...");break;
    case FRIDAY: System.out.println("Thank you God, it is Friday!");break;
    case SATURDAY: case SUNDAY: System.out.println("Relax and enjoy your Weekend!");break;
    default: System.out.println("Work, what else?");break;
}
```

Statement Return Boolean Result

If you have a statement like this:

```
If (a>10){
    return true;
} else {
    return false;
}
```

The simple equivalent of this statement could be:

```
return (a>10);
```

Use Operator '?' When Possible

If you have a statement similar to this:

```
If (a>10){
    b=c;
} else {
    b=d;
}
```

Its compact equivalent statement is:

```
b = (a>10)?c:d;
```

Handle Exceptions

You have to wrap the exceptions in your application in 'try..catch' to handle them. If you leave them unhandled, they can be thrown and hang the system to cause a denial of service. But, if you developed your code to be a library, for example, your code must allow the exception to be thrown on the stack. That allows the higher level (the caller) to see the problem to handle it properly.

The second point is never to leave the catch block empty. Because if you do it and an exception is thrown while running your program, debugging will be difficult and time-consuming to figure out what the problem is because it is kept out of sight.

Strings Concatenation

Using the + operator is an inefficient way to concatenate multiple strings because the Java compiler will create many String objects to store intermediate results before the last outcome. That causes a waste of memory and processing time. To avoid such a situation, you can use the built-in 'StringBuilder', which is mutable. Thus, the compiler will not create additional intermediate variables to store the partial results. Let's take an example of string concatenation in Java:

```java
String sql = "SELECT * FROM Customers";
sql += " WHERE CustomerFName = '" + user.getFirstName() + "'";
sql += " AND CustomerLName = '" + user.getLastName() + "'";
sql += " AND CustomerEmail = '" + user.getEmail() + "'";
```

You can rewrite this code using 'StringBuilder' to look like this:

```java
StringBuilder sb = new StringBuilder("SELECT * FROM Customers");
sb.append("               WHERE               CustomerFName               =
'").append(user.getFirstName()).append("'");
sb.append("               AND               CustomerLName               =
'").append(user.getLastName()).append("'");
sb.append(" AND CustomerEmail = '").append(user.getEmail()).append("'");
String sql = sb.toString();
```

Equality between Objects

Be careful when using object equality in Java. If 'a' and 'b' are objects, you cannot use equality like this:

```java
if (a==b) {
//do something
}
```

The equality ('==') is reserved for primary types. The correct way to do this is to use the equals method of the Objects class:

```java
if (Objects.equals(a, b)){
//do something
}
```

Or you can do it like this:

```java
if (a.equals(b)){
//do something
```

```
}
```

But, in this case, you have to be sure that 'a' is not null.

A special case of equality between two objects is when one of them is a not-null constant:

```
final static String STATIC_CODE = "Success";
```

It's better when you start with the constant like this:

```
if (STATIC_CODE.equals(obj)){
//....
}
```

Because if you start with a nullable object like this:

```
if (obj.equals(STATIC_CODE)){
//....
}
```

Then an exception can be thrown. But, the former statement will be executed safely.

For-Loop

Avoid using the old form of the for-loop:

```
for (int i = 0; i < arr.length; i++) {
    method1(names[i]);
}
```

The index can be changed incidentally. You can go wrong and start the index from 1 instead of 0, which can corrupt the result of executing the loop. To avoid such issues, especially when you don't need the index, you can use the improved for-loop like this:

```
for (String item: arr) {
    method1(item);
}
```

Use of Functional Programming

The latest versions of Java support functional programming paradigms, which allows you to do better than using the for-loop when required. The functional programming style reduces code complexity, making it precise, predictable, easier to test, shorter, more understandable, and readable. Let's see this through an example that compares imperative and functional paradigms in Java. In this example, we want to filter a list of integers to keep only even numbers and then find the maximum value.

List<Integer> nums = Arrays.asList(10, 15, -36, 25, 30, 75, 102, -50, 220, 100, 502);

An imperative code of such a program might look like this:

```java
int max = 0;
for (Integer n: nums) {
    if (n%2==0) {
        if (max<n){
            max = n;
        }
    }
}
System.out.println(max);
```

The code mentioned above will be rewritten in a single line by using the functional style

```java
System.out.println(nums.stream().filter(n->n%2==0).max(Integer::compare).orElse(0));
```

All the steps are chained one after the other. We filter the stream of 'nums' to obtain only the even numbers. Next, we apply the max function on the result (result stream of filter) with an integer comparator to get the max among the even numbers. As 'max' returns an optional integer, we apply 'orElse' to return 0 if no max is returned.

Useless Objects

Creating objects in Java is memory and processor-consuming. So, only create objects when you need them. An example of creating unnecessary objects is using constructors to instantiate string objects like this:

```java
String str = new String("Hello World!");
```

That is useless. The initialization should be done directly like this:

```java
String str = "Hello World!";
```

Returning Empty Collection

When you have a method that returns a collection as its result, and in some cases, it returns a null value, it is better to return an empty collection rather than a null value. That is because null elements require extra checking work to prevent a null exception from being thrown.

Optional Class

Optional is a container object that can include a null value. That helps reduce null checks. The Optional class has methods that help make programs shorter and easier to understand. We suggest an example to explain it. We have a method named 'isAlpha' with an optional string as a parameter. The expected string is a sequence of characters separated by semicolons (;). The 'isAlpha' method splits the 'str' parameter to get the words. It checks for each word if it contains only alphabetic characters to return true.

```java
public static boolean isAlpha(Optional<String> str) {
    String words[] = str.orElse("").split(";");
    return Arrays.stream(words).allMatch(x -> StringUtils.isAlpha(x));
}
```

We can call this method from the main method as follows:

```java
public static void main(String[] args) {
    String str = args.length>0?args[0]:null;
    System.out.println(isAlpha(Optional.ofNullable(str)));
}
```

There is no null check throughout the code. That makes it smaller and more intuitive. The code works correctly even for null values.

Memory Leaks

Memory management in Java is automatic, and developers have no control over it. But, they can follow some best practices to reduce the risk of getting memory leaks. As a sign of poor quality code, a memory leak is a bad situation where the garbage collector cannot remove unused objects. So, they stay in memory indefinitely. Therefore, the space allocated to the application will be smaller and smaller until raising OutOfMemoryError and disturbing the normal execution of your application. That will question the reliability of your application. You can get notified that an application is experiencing a memory leak if its performance continuously decreases or its memory usage increases during its running.

Best Practices to Preventing Memory Leak

You can follow a few rules when programming to limit the risk of memory leaks in Java:

- Avoid creating unnecessary objects.

- Use String Builder instead of string concatenation.

- Avoid storing a massive volume of data during a session.

- Keep the timeout low for each session and invalidate it when no longer needed.

- Don't use static objects too much, as they live as long as the application itself.

- Release closable resources like database connection objects in final blocks or when you no longer need them.

4.3. Best Practices in JQuery

As with Java, we want more best practices and recommendations, but this time for JQuery. This language is one of the most popular programming languages in the world and is widely used as it is one of the paramount technologies of the World Wide Web.

Shorter Condition Checking

JQuery has a short way to write condition-checking logic. For example, instead of writing something like this:

```
if (data){
    console.log(data.id);
}
```

You can write it simply like that:

```
data && console.log(data.id);
```

You can convert multiple lines of code like:

```
var id = null;
if (data){
    id = data.id;
}
```

To one line to do the same job:

```
var id = data && data.id;
```

If you have a statement like this:

```
if (a<b) {
    return -1;
} else if (a>b) {
    return 1;
} else {
    return 0;
}
```

You can write it like that:

```
return a<b?1 : a > b ? -1 : 0;
```

This statement is usually used to sort an array of comparables.

If you have a statement like this:
```
if (x != null){
    z = x;
} else {
    z = y;
}
```
In a simpler and shorter way, write it like this:
```
z = x || y;
```

Enhanced For -Loop
In JQuery also, you can skip using the for-loop with index:
```
for (var i=0;i<arr.length;i++){
    let item = arr[i];
    //Rest of the code
}
```
So, use the enhanced for-loop as follows if you want to iterate through items:
```
for (let item of arr){
    //Rest of the code
}
```

But, if you want to iterate over the index of the array, you can do it like this:
```
for (let index in arr){
    //Rest of the code
}
```

Functional Programming in JQuery
JQuery provides several functions for iterating over collections of data (for example, arrays) like each, forEach, filter, map, and reduce. When possible, use these functions instead of the for-loop. These functions have a shorter intuitive syntax and are more readable and understandable. Here we give the filter and join functions as examples.

Filter
This function selects items from an array. These items should match a specific condition. The following example uses this function to filter an array of objects to get those named 'Helene' and under 30 years old.
```
var persons = [];
persons.push({ name: "John", age:30});
persons.push({ name: "Helene", age:25});
persons.push({ name: "Nadia", age:45});
```

```
var filteredPers = persons.filter(function(obj) {
    return (obj.name === "Helene") && (obj.age < 30);
});

$.each(filteredPers, function(i, elem) {
    alert(elem.name);
    //Rest of the code
});
```

Join

This function joins all the elements of an array with a separator. In our example below, we concatenate the words of the 'arr' array using the comma as a separator. The corresponding statement is simple and compact. You don't need to iterate over the array items and do extra work to perform such an operation.

```
var arr = ["Hello", "World!"];
$(".mydiv").text( arr.join( ", "));
```

Operations on Set of Elements

Don't try to iterate over a set of items to act if it's simple enough to do so on the set. Suppose you want to change the color of all items in a set. If you're iterating through the elements of the set, you may do it like this:

```
$("li").map(function() {
    $(this).css("background-color", "grey");
});
```

You can act on the entire set in one go:

```
$("li").css("background-color", "grey");
```

It is a shorter, straighter, and better practice.

Set Operators

You should note that 'set operators' are sometimes sufficient to obtain the desired result instead of explicitly writing a logic. Let's take an example to explain this approach. Suppose we want to write a function that retrieves an 'info' data attribute from any element of the 'mydiv' class. For this, we suggest the following logic-based code:

```
function getData() {
    var $mydiv = $('.mydiv');
    if ($mydiv.length > 0) {
        return $mydiv.data('info');
    } else {
        return undefined;
```

```
        }
}
```

A better practice is to use 'set operators' like this:
```
function getData() {
    return $('.mydiv').data('info');
}
```

It is not necessary to check whether the element exists or whether the data attribute exists. Such checking is implicitly integrated into the statement $('.mydiv').data('info').

Element Existence Checking
A way to check if an element exists is to use its length:
```
if ($("selector").length) {
    //..
}
```

Actions Chaining
If you need to get elements and apply a series of actions to them, you can do it one after the other in multiple statements like this:
```
var $div = $('.mydiv');
$div.addClass('a-class');
$div.css('color','red');
$div.css('background','yellow');
$div.width('250px');
$div.removeClass('b-class');
$div.slideUp(2000);
$div.slideDown(2000);
```

But, a better practice in JQuery is to use the chaining to execute a set of methods on a set of elements. The syntax is shorter and more intuitive:
```
$('.mydiv')
    .addClass('a-class').css('color','red')
    .css('background','yellow').width('250px')
    .removeClass('another-class')
    .slideUp(2000).slideDown(2000);
```

Handling Multiple Events
If you have the situation to handle multiple events for a set of elements, the simplest way to do it is to handle each event like this:
```
$('.mydiv').on('mouseenter',function() {
```

```
    //Handle mouseenter event
});
$('.mydiv').on('mouseleave',function(){
    //Handle mouseleave event
});
$('.mydiv').on('click',function(){
    //Handle click event
});
```

A better solution consists of grouping all the functions to handle the different events under one action for the same set of elements:

```
$('.mydiv').on({
    'mouseenter': function(){
        //Handle mouseenter event
    },
    'mouseleave': function(){
        //Handle mouseleave event
    },
    'click': function(){
        //Handle click event
    }
});
```

Navigating to DOM

Using selectors to navigate to a DOM is a common practice in JQuery. Such statements can affect the performance of your code if they are done randomly. The use, for example, of universal selectors can increase the navigation time. But, using a specific selector like Id, the query time decreases. For example, carrying out a search using the following selector is expensive:

```
$("table > *")
```

But the following solution is more precise:

```
$("table .myclass")
```

There are good practices to follow to make navigation to a DOM more effective. We mention some of them here.

Using Id

It is good to use the Id selector to find an element and to go up or down using .children(), .find(), .parent(), ...

If you have this statement:

```
$('#mydiv > .child').css({color: 'grey'});
```

It is better to write it like this:
```
$('#mydiv')
  .children('.child')
  .css({color: 'grey'});
```

Filtering in CSS

Filter early in CSS to avoid creating unnecessary objects in memory. For example when you have a statement like this:
```
var first = $('.mydiv').first();
```
The expression $('.mydiv') will create an object for each element found. The expression 'first()' will seek the first element among those found to create a new object for it. But a better solution could look like this:
```
var first = $('.mydiv:first');
```

In this solution, only the first found of elements matching '.mydiv' will be created in memory.

Restricting Searching Start Point

If possible, search only the part of the document you need by looking for the descendants of the known elements. It is faster and more efficient than parsing the entire document. In the following example, it is not recommended to start from the whole document:
```
$.find("ul").css("background-color", "grey");
```

You can precise your ancestor like this:
```
$("ul").children('li').css("background-color", "grey");
```

Reuse References

Do not look for the same components more than once. You should store the elements found in a variable to use them later. So you will no longer need to look for them. If you have a snippet of code similar to this example:
```
$("div.p").addClass("cl-a");
$("div.p span").addClass("cl-b");
```

A best practice is to reuse the ancestor you find by storing it in a variable like this:
```
$mydiv = $("div.p").addClass("cl-a");
$mydiv.find("span").addClass("cl-b");
```

References

[1] Jim kwik, 'Limitless'. Hay house, INC, 2020.

[2] B. J Fogg. Tiny Habits: The Small Changes That Change Everything. Houghton Mifflin Harcourt Publishing, 2020.

[3] James Clear. Atomic Habits: An Easy & Proven Way to Build Good Habits & Break Bad Ones. 375 Hudson Street New York, 2018.

[4] Robert C. Martin, 'Agile Software Development, Principles, Patterns, and Practices'. Pearson Education Limited 2014.

[5] Robert C. Martin, 'Design Principles and Design Patterns'. By Robert C. Martin, 2000.

[6] Erich Gamma, Richard Helm, Ralph Johnson and John Vlissides. 'Design Patterns: Elements of Reusable Object-Oriented Software'. Addison-Wesley Professional Computing Series, ISBN 0-201- 63448-2, 1995.

[7] https://wiki.sei.cmu.edu/confluence/display/java/SEI+CERT+Oracle+Coding+Standard+for+Java

[8] UNICODE NORMALIZATION FORMS. Technical Reports. http://www.unicode.org/reports/tr15/tr15-23.html

[9] Intellij Idea. https://www.jetbrains.com/help/idea/getting-started.html

[10] Visual Studio Code. https://visualstudio.microsoft.com/vs/features/

[11] Notepad++ User Manual. https://npp-user-manual.org/

[12] Java Documentation. https://docs.oracle.com/en/java/

[13] Chrome DevTools. https://developer.chrome.com/docs/devtools/

[14] Tabnine. https://www.tabnine.com/

[15] SonarLint. https://www.sonarlint.org/

[16] https://www.hsph.harvard.edu/nutritionsource/healthy-eating-plate/

[17] Healthy Diet. World Health Organization. https://www.who.int/news-room/fact-sheets/detail/healthy-diet

[18] Physical Activity. World Health Organization. https://www.who.int/news-room/fact-sheets/detail/physical-activity.